Marriage Supper Of The Lamb

And End Time Events

Messages For This Last Generation
Dictated To Susan Davis

From The Heart of GOD

D1416576

WORDS FROM THE HEART OF GOD

NOTE FROM THE AUTHOR

This book was not created for the generation of profit but for the purpose of reaching more people through this particular medium. But certainly not to raise money through the use of these prophetic Words of the LORD. The list price of this book was set to cover only printing costs and the royalty that goes to the author is near zero. (There may be a few cents per book due to fluctuating printing costs. Any remainder over zero is used to buy books which are given away for free.) These messages are so urgent and important that we want to ensure that the price of the book would not be an obstacle to people getting these messages.

WORDS FROM THE HEART OF GOD

ABOUT THESE PROPHECIES

Susan operates in the gift of prophecy. In 1 Corinthians 14:1 it states, "Follow the way of love and eagerly desire gifts of the Spirit, especially prophecy." Now we are living and supposed to be obeying God's instructions in the New Testament. Although some believe that spiritual gifts, such as prophecies, have been done away with, this is man's thinking and not God's. God has not changed His covenant. We are still living in the era of the New Covenant – which is also called the New Testament. Please understand that your first commitment should be to the Lord Jesus Christ and His Word as written in the Bible – especially the New Testament.

As always, all prophecy needs to be tested against the Bible. However, if the prophecy lines up with the Bible then we are expected to obey it. Currently God does not use prophecies to introduce new doctrines. They are used to reinforce what God has already given to us in the Bible. God also uses them to give us individual warnings of future events that will affect us.

Just like in the Old Testament, God uses prophets in the New Testament times of which we are currently in. The book of Acts, which is in the New Testament, mentions some of the prophets such as Judas and Silas (Acts 15:32) and Agabus (Acts 21:21) and there were others. The ministry of prophets is also mentioned in New Testament times in 1 Corinthians 12:28, 14:1,29,32,37 as well as in Ephesians 2:20,3:5,4:11.

Jesus chooses prophets to work for Him on earth. Among other things, Jesus uses prophecies and prophets to communicate His desires to His children. The Bible itself was written prophetically through the inspiration of the Holy Spirit.

Some people say words of prophecy are in danger of adding to the Bible or taking from it -- well the Bible speaks of prophecy as being a Gift of the HOLY SPIRIT. The way the Bible is added to or taken from is not through additional words of prophecy received by the people which the HOLY SPIRIT gives words to, but by the changing of GOD's concepts to add new unBiblical concepts from other pagan beliefs for example. But the primary work of the prophets in the Bible has always been to focus the people back to GOD's WORD, the BIBLE.

As it says in 1 Thessalonians 5:19-21, "Do not put out the Spirit's fire; do not treat prophecies with contempt. Test everything. Hold on to the good." And the way to test the messages is to compare it's content to what the Bible says.

In all the prophecies below I personally (Mike Peralta - Book Preparer) have tested these messages and they are all in agreement to what the Bible says. But you must also test these messages, yourself, to the Bible. And if they are consistent with the Bible, then God expects that you will take them to heart and obey His instructions.

TABLE OF CONTENTS

INTRODUCTION BY THE LORD

MY children, this is your LORD Speaking. I am coming very soon. MY Coming is near, even at the door. I am coming! You need to make ready.

This journal was completed during a 40-day fast by MY daughter Susan. She did this fast at MY Request. I brought her to a secluded location so that she might die to herself. During this time, I gave her many Words that I wanted to go out to MY children. So she wrote MY Words as I led her. All these Letters have important information you need to read and consider, as MY Coming is near.

This is your LORD and SAVIOR, YAHUSHUA (Jesus Christ).

*All scripture included comes from the King James Version Bible

These Words were dictated by GOD The FATHER and HIS SON, YAHUSHUA HA MASHIACH [Jesus Christ or Jesus The Anointed or Jesus The Messiah] to Susan during a forty-day fast recorded between January 27, 2012 through March 6, 2012.

TESTIMONIALS

I thank you so much for your e-mails and sharing GOD's Words and it blessed me so much. I prayed and asked the HOLY SPIRIT to guide me to make me understand many things and to walk in HIS Way. Please pray for me also. Once again thank you so much and GOD bless you and your ministry. – Reader 1

* * * * * *

Dear, Dear Sister Susan, Thank You YAHUSHUA for these letters and what YOU asked YOUR daughter/bride to go through so they could be written! I began the day after and read about ten pages each time. I am blessed. – Reader 2

* * * * * *

Susan, thank you so much for the link you shared. It is absolutely blessed me and I feel my spirit so hungry to the LORD YAHUSHUA. – Reader 3

* * * * * *

Hello My Dear Sister Susan, I am almost finished reading GOD's Messages/Letters to you during your fast. They are truly HIS WORDS... I mean I just cannot put that 100-page document down. HIS Truth, Wisdom, and pleading with us is amazing...HE is just so humble and loving to be able to encourage, warn the nations. I thank HIM for it, and bless you for sharing it with me. – Reader 4

* * * * * *

Dear Susan, Thank you, my dear sister, for sending this to me! I posted it, and I am already halfway through. It brought me to my knees before the LORD. I pray that millions will do the same. May GOD bless you for your obedience and faithfulness to HIM. Love forever in our MESSIAH! – Reader 5

* * * * * *

Susan, this is an extremely anointed prophecy from the Lord. I have heard prophecies from the time I was a baby Christian back in 1979. I have heard and read some very anointed prophecies over the past 33 years and the messages in this book are of the most anointed I have heard and read in all my life. – Mike Peralta (Book Preparer)

WORDS FROM THE HEART OF GOD

CHAPTER 1

HUMILITY

Humility is humble submission. It is a willingness to serve others without complaint, to overlook harm from others with a smile and forgiveness. It is a desire to serve others and to please GOD. It is a desire to serve GOD at all times with hopeful expectations, to be compliant, a willing spirit always ready to serve GOD and others. Humility is also willing to take a back seat - the last chair, the furthest position, to be in the background, to be unnoticed.

Luke 14:7-12. And he put forth a parable to those which were bidden, when he marked how they chose out the chief rooms; saying unto them, When thou art bidden of any man to a wedding, sit not down in the highest room; lest a more honorable man than thou be bidden of him; And he that bade thee and him come and say to thee, Give this man place; and thou begin with shame to take the lowest room. But when thou art bidden, go and sit down in the lowest room; that when thou art bidden, go and sit down in the lowest room; that when he that bade thee cometh, he may say unto thee, Friend, go up higher: then shalt thou have worship in the presence of them that sit at meat with thee. For whosoever exalteth himself shall be abased; and he that humbleth himself shall be exalted.

Matthew 19:30. But many that are first shall be last; and the last shall be first.

It is the person who is forgotten because they are so lowly, they blend into the scenery. They do not want center stage. They want to be hidden away, quiet, unassuming, submissive to GOD. This is humility, daughter and this is MY bride.

She is all these things. Do you see your errors now daughter? Let US continue... What is being humble? It is working behind the scenes but not desiring the lime light. It is complete submission to GOD. It is seeking to obey GOD in all things.

Humility is not worrying about what other people think of you. It is doing for others without receiving credit. It is desiring favor from GOD and not men. It is growing in favor with GOD and pleasing GOD.

It is quiet and unassuming.

It is growing in GOD.

It is being "CHRIST-like." Humility is most beautiful to GOD. A humble, GOD-fearing person shines in GOD's Eyes.

Humility is wanting to please GOD and walk in His Path. To be lowly and not think well of yourself and to not think yourself better than others, to consider yourself below others, and to not judge those around you. I am the only ONE to judge. It does not mean you are to be abased. It means you are to respect others' feelings even if they stumble and not to belittle them in your heart, to have compassion for them because you too are not beyond sinning before a Holy GOD.

This is what happens when someone is humble. They create a wonderful testimony. They shine in MY Kingdom, in MY Eyes. They receive the Ear of GOD. I listen to MY humble servants when they cry out to ME. I would go to any extreme to save MY humble servants. I will move heaven and earth for MY humble servants. Do you understand this, MY daughter? MY humble servants are devoted to ME. They understand that they cannot do anything without ME. They are always seeking ME in all ways like a child seeks its parent. This is MY humble servant. They have no self will. They trust only ME in their daily walk. They search ME for their answers. They trust ME wholeheartedly and I answer them. I give them MY Best because they seek ME above all others for answers. They are humble and glorious in MY Sight. They have a soft-spoken beauty about them. They are not like the world around them.

They stand out from the crowd. Their beauty is GOD-like and heavenly. This is how heaven is - full of people secure in their GOD because I meet all their needs.

6

There is no need to be brash or rude, arrogant or prideful. All their needs are met through ME. They are content, willing to serve, and happy to serve because I fulfill all their needs, all the time. No one vies for attention in MY heavenlies.

Everyone is content. It is a place of purity, peace, calm, love, laughter, joy.

Childlike faith is important because a child does not get ahead of itself. A child follows close behind its parent because it trusts the parent. It clings to the parent with hopeful expectation waiting for instruction, guidance, leadership. The child does not assume the role of parent. It knows better. It cannot lead; it trusts only the parent to meet all of its needs. When the child gets out of sight of the parent, panic sets in because it knows all its needs are met in the parent it has grown to love and trust. This is the relationship between the truly humble and GOD. The humble follow GOD blindly out of trust and obedience and GOD delivers them.

There are not answers anywhere else. GOD is Supreme and the only True Hope, Reliable Hope.

Children seek their parents for all their needs. They cry after them because their parents can deliver them just as GOD delivers the humble who follow HIM from a humble, pure heart.

Is this making sense to you now daughter? Can a person full of pride change their ways and become humble? Daughter, the answer is "yes" by the guidance and submission to ME, your GOD.

So with GOD all things are possible? Yes, all things are possible with ME!

Proverbs 15:33. The fear of the LORD is the instruction of wisdom; and before honor is humility.

Let US begin. Humility is about love. Love comes from a heart of humility. Love does not come from pride. Pride destroys love. Pride says: "I am better than you;" "I know more than you;" "You are worth

7

less than ME;" "You are valueless to ME;" "I am self- sufficient;" and "I do not need you." This is what pride stands for, MY child.

Pride is ugly in all forms. It is self-seeking, self-centered, selfish, and its roots are evil. Vain glory rises up against GOD and says: "I don't need GOD." I am MY own god - I rule myself. It is ugly and abominable. There is no beauty in this. There is nothing redeeming in this. It puts others off. It causes people to feel inferior, rejected, unloved, offended, hurt. There is nothing remotely GOD-like in pride and it is the opposite of the characteristic of CHRIST. There is nothing CHRIST- like in pride. Nothing good comes from pride - only evil. Do you understand, MY child? How can we flee from the appearance of pride, LORD? Daughter, you must run from pride, run far from it. Seek humility at all times.

Daughter, there is no need to build yourself up to seek the attention of others if you have MY Love and Affection.

Seek MY Love and Affection and be satisfied in it only and all desires to seek love from those around you will be eclipsed by MY all-consuming love. The people around you cannot gratify your deepest needs - only I can do this for you. Only I can satisfy the hungry, longing, empty heart.

I have all the answers for the longing, empty heart. I can fill all longings. Men cannot. They are not capable although it appears that way. There is only short- lived and brief gratification from the approval of others. I am the wellspring that fills to completion. I fill and satisfy all the longings of the human heart. Come to ME to satisfy your need for love and affection. Lay down pride. It is a destructive force and has no love. It operates outside of love and only brings destruction to everyone. Pride is the first evil. Still it rules and reigns in men's hearts. Pride causes men to seek after all ways contrary to seeking GOD.

Men build themselves up by position in their work, talents, wealth, possessions, and relationships with others. These are idols and they do not set their sights on GOD for their answers, only to build themselves up through pursuits that I do not ordain, so that they can appear successful to those around them. Only the humble-hearted pursue GOD for their answers and needs and put aside their desire to pursue the things to impress those around them.

When you try to amass wealth or make a name for yourself in the world - even through ministry work, it is you striving to be accepted by others, to seek approval from those around you. This is not MY Will. It cannot be. MY humble children seek ME for their needs daily and I deliver them. This is how I teach trust for GOD.

When MY children strive in their own power and succeed, they are failing because I will not reward those who are out of MY Will although things look well and good, it is false security.

And I also allow MY children to fail in their strivings so they see they need ME. I need to be the desire of the heart and the answer to everything. Everything else is false hope, leading MY children out of MY Will.

Yes these are prideful children seeking their own way apart from consulting ME and knowing and trusting ME. This leads to inferior satisfaction. Strive and strive, MY children strive and only come up empty longing for more, never really satiated - always wanting more, but not knowing what. I am that "WHAT!" I am the only way to true satisfaction, to a whole heart, whole spirit, whole soul.

I satisfy, I complete, I make whole, I fill the voids of the human heart's longings, nothing or no one else. This is the basis of pride and the sin that stems from it, an ever-seeking heart looking for gratification and approval in everything but GOD. Empty, lonely, and unfulfilled is the ultimate outcome, a sad existence that I never meant for MY creation.

Pride, an ugly sin that is completely devoid of love in any form, a loveless position holds no love for anyone. Humility by contrast loves. It is not self-serving. It does not rule over others. It waits for others to be served first. It holds others in higher esteem than itself. It does not take advantage. It is not rude or arrogant.

It is not haughty. It does not put on airs. It does not flaunt. It is beautiful, soft- spoken, sweet-natured, loving, caring, GOD-like, CHRIST-like, GOD-seeking.

It does not rule over others or force its position. It is only concerned for the positions of others. This is humility, always in the background, never vying for first chair. This is MY Way - patient and resilient.

Humility is a form of love. It does not impose itself on others. It waits its turn. It loves above all else. It does not seek to abase others to be lifted up. It only seeks good for those around.

Why is humility a beautiful thing to ME, GOD? I am pleased when MY children humble themselves before ME. It is a show of honor, respect, and trust in ME, their GOD. They put all their hopes and expectations on ME to fulfill all their needs. They remove their desire to seek themselves for answers through their own accomplishments, their own strength, their own self-seeking will. They are not inclined to follow their own heart, abandon ME, their GOD, focus on their own selfish pursuits which leads them away from the One True Way; ME, their GOD. I am the only Way, Truth, Path.

Many are deceived by pursuing their own ways apart from coming close to ME and seeking MY Will, MY Truth, and MY Direction for their life.

They pursue what the world says is right: seeking money, position, fame, and satisfaction in a myriad of ways apart from ME, GOD. This is high class deception.

I am not saying that you should not work or live life, but I am saying to seek ME first and I can direct the right path to take as you live in this world. If you pursue your plans and dreams apart from MY Intervention then you are running outside of MY Will and you leave yourself open to MY enemy and you are living in sin because you are not in MY Will. This is pride and rebellion. Many walk in it.

Proverbs 18:12. Before destruction the heart of man is haughty, and before honor is humility.

Proverbs 29:23. A man's pride shall bring him low: but honor shall uphold the humble in spirit.

Matthew 23:12. And whosoever shall exalt himself shall be abased; and he that humble himself shall be exalted.

James 4:6. But He giveth more grace. Wherefore he saith, GOD resisteth the proud, but giveth grace unto the humble.

Proverbs 8:13. The fear of the LORD is to hate evil: pride, and arrogancy, and the evil way, and the forward mouth do I hate.

How does one stay in your Will, LORD? This is how to stay in MY Will: submit yourself to ME - complete surrender. Then I guide your steps. This is daily. Coming to ME each day and asking for direction, guidance, like a child. This is childlike faith. The world has painted a picture that being self-sufficient is the way to a successful life. It is a well-plotted plan of deception from MY enemy. He has deceived the world with this lie. MY children pursue life through their own, thought-out planning and schemes, never once consulting ME, their MAKER and they believe all is well. If it looks right, it must be right. But it is evil meant to throw MY children off the narrow path. Only I have the right course, the right way for MY children to walk in and this course I give them each day.

John 5:30. I can of MINE OWN SELF do nothing: as I hear, I judge: and MY judgment is just; because I seek not MINE OWN will, but the Will of the FATHER which hath sent ME.

If people have to live in this world sometime they are forced to plan ahead, what about that? My child, yes MY children live in the world, but I even can give direction about the choices made for the future. If MY children seek ME, sometimes the answer is: "Be still and wait." Only MY children, who are intentionally close to ME, walk with ME daily, will be given this insight. When MY children are far from ME and only come to ME occasionally, this I will not bless. I am not a GOD WHO you can check in with every now and then, as so many children believe. Many come to ME during their crisis and then they go back to forgetting ME. These children do not know ME.

I am a GOD who desires intimacy, closeness with MY children. This is evil to ME...lukewarm, to which I spit out.

Luke 7:21-23. Not everyone that saith unto ME, LORD, LORD, have we not prophesied in THY Name? And in THY Name have cast out devils? And in THY Name done many wonderful works? And then will I profess unto them, I never knew you: depart from ME, ye that work iniquity.

CHAPTER 2

DO NOT TRUST YOURSELF OR OTHERS

Now daughter, Let US begin. Today, I want to discuss with you about the problem with trusting in "self." Being self-sufficient, self-reliant and self-centered is an evil vice. It is promoted by the world system and fostered by MY enemy.

Being self-reliant is nothing more than putting "self" before GOD. It is walking in your own will apart from MY Will. Just like this 40-day fast is MY Will, when people do what they choose without seeking ME through an intimate relationship with ME, they run apart from MY Will and they are living in sin - it is rebellion to ME. I want MY children to walk in MY Will. Sometimes MY Will does not look right according to the standards of the world. The world says chase money, possessions, security, human love. MY Will doesn't match what the world calls normal. It looks different. But MY Will is correct.

I created humans and I also created them to trust ME and walk in MY Will - to know MY Will you must lay down your life before ME in humble submission and seek ME daily. Those who truly pursue ME by devoting time to ME, intimate time with ME in the secret place and reading MY Word will find ME and MY Will. This requires choices. You must choose because worldly distractions can throw you off MY straight and narrow path. O' there are many other paths to go on but all lead to destruction as the road to hell is a broad road that many fall into. Few find this important narrow path to ME and eternal life. Many think they walk the narrow path but they are deceived. They listen to others who are also deceived.

Many of MY leaders are deceived and deceiving others because they believe doing many works and staying busy in MY churches is the way to eternal security but this is deception. It is only by intimacy, truly knowing ME, spending time, devoting time to knowing ME. This is the key to eternal safety and security.

Psalms 91:1. He that dwelleth in the secret place of the MOST HIGH shall abide under the shadow of the ALMIGHTY The body is fed in the churches but this body cannot truly function correctly apart from nourishment which I give in the secret place and in the time spent getting to know ME in a deep way. This is where the body is truly built up. This is where I deliver MY Will and Words to MY sheep and sustain them to survive what the enemy tries to do to cause trouble. It is by intimacy with ME that you can sustain through the pitfalls and trials of life. If you go it alone you will struggle and ultimately fail. Because you do not know what I require apart from ME and I am the ultimate judge of all in the end.

How can you prepare to face ME in judgment if you have never come close to ME and learned what I desire and require of you? When you face ME without this intimacy you will be empty-handed because you have relied on your own beliefs, own thinking, own will, and you will fall greatly short. You will miss the mark.

Romans 14:12. So then every one of us shall give account of himself to GOD.

Don't be deceived. Many of MY so-called leaders never spend time with ME, and they too do not operate in MY Will, and they are as if the blind leading the blind down blind alleys of destruction. Many will be surprised how misled they have been because they have trusted in those who know ME not and they themselves are greatly deceived.

You cannot trust in what looks right in the world. You must submit to ME.

Surrender your all to ME and seek ME whole-heartedly. This is what I require.

MY Word speaks this Truth. Read it correctly and see for yourself. MY leaders, too many like the world and its ways, so they change the meaning of MY Words so they can feel good about mingling with the world. The world is an enmity to ME. Read MY Word. This truth is not hidden. You cannot love the world and ME both. I have been clear about this. O' yes you are in the world, but you must follow ME and MY Ways while you are in the world.

James 4:4. Ye adulterers and adulteresses know ye not that the friendship of the world is enmity with GOD? Whosoever therefore will be a friend of the world is an enemy of GOD.

There are distractions at every turn that will lead you away from seeking intimacy with ME. You must desire to spend time with ME more than the world's distractions. You are settling for an inferior, empty pursuit if you settle for the things of the world over a relationship with the CREATOR of all life - your MAKER, MAKER of the stars, and the heavens.

Hebrews 10:38-39. Now the just shall live by faith: but if any man draws back, MY soul shall have no pleasure in him. But we are not of them who draw back unto perdition; but of them that believe to the saving of the soul.

Do not trade down a glorious eternal walk with ME, the CREATOR and SUSTAINER of all life for the cheap thrills offered by the world. What you pursue in the world is empty satisfaction and ultimately death. You choose your own destiny, you believe you create your own path, you believe I bless your decisions. You have not come to know ME intimately. If you did, you would learn differently. You are deceived by the ways of the world and MY cunning enemy. He would have you do what you believe best for yourself apart from ME. This I cannot bless. Then MY children wonder why they run into so many troubles. The worst deception of MY enemy is the belief that all is well when you run apart from having an intimate relationship with ME. This is the greatest deception of all. All seems well, but when you face ME, I will tell you to depart ye workers of iniquity, I never knew you...

Matthew 7:21. Not everyone that saith unto ME, LORD, LORD, shall enter into the Kingdom of Heaven; but he that doeth the Will of MY FATHER which is in Heaven.

Many will say to ME in that day, LORD, LORD, have we not prophesied in THY Name? And in THY Name have cast out devils? And in THY Name done many wonderful works? And then will I profess unto them, I never knew you. depart from ME, ye that work iniquity.

Yes, this is MY Word. I did not create you to walk apart from ME and for you to seek your own way without ever consulting ME. Yes, you can do these things because you have free will, but you are not in MY Will and so you are sinning against ME.

I give MY children free will and they can choose to seek ME in intimacy and trust MY Guidance or they can run apart from ME. When MY children run apart from ME, out of MY Will, seeking their own plans, they work against MY Kingdom plans and this is evil. They cause destruction they don't even know about, because they have selfishly believed they can live their life outside of MY Perfect Will and Plans.

They bring trouble on themselves and others. They leave themselves open the whims and traps of the enemy. Children apart from ME, you are no match to the wiles and cunning of MY enemy. Do not think yourself so wise. You are useless apart from ME.

Why do I talk so of those with childlike faith as the ones who will inherit MY Kingdom? Because these children recognize their need for ME at every turn just as a child turns to its parent at every moment. The child knows apart from the parent he is in danger as MY children recognize apart from ME, they too are in great danger, and trust in MY Every Word. This is why I implore MY children to spend time in MY Word, where much information is imparted. All answers for living this life are given in MY Book. I gave this Book as a guide for mankind.

MY SPIRIT reveals truth in the pages. Only through surrender and receiving MY SPIRIT in full measure will you receive the enlightenment that you need to truly understand MY Words. It is not by the teachings of men, but by MY SPIRIT that the Words grow in your heart. Only by MY SPIRIT can you receive the light-giving life of MY Book.

Matthew 18:4. Whosoever therefore shall humble himself as this little child, the same is greatest in the kingdom of heaven.

1 Corinthians 2:11-14. For what man knoweth the things of a man, save the spirit of man which is in him? Even so the things of GOD knoweth no man, but the SPIRIT of GOD. Now we have received, not the spirit of the world, but the SPIRIT which is of GOD; that we might know the things that are freely given to us of GOD.

Which things also we speak, not in the words which man's wisdom teacheth, but which the HOLY GHOST teacheth; comparing Spiritual things with Spiritual.

But the natural man receiveth not the things of the SPIRIT of GOD: for they are foolishness unto him: neither can he know them, because they are Spiritually discerned.

The world is full of deception now. Don't be fooled by the evil propagated by MY enemy. He would have you believe by the messages you receive daily that you can trust the things of the world. You trust in everything but ME, the GIVER of life. You trust in money, education, worldly security, governments - it is false help and security. This is high class deception and it leads MY children away from ME. MY children then dabble in trusting ME.

They turn to ME a little and then rely on everything else. This is not intimacy.

Yes, you are intimate with the world and your own desires, but not with ME. You need to come to ME and lay everything down before ME. You cannot truly know ME until you put aside your worldly security and come to ME seeking an intimate relationship. Anything else apart from this relationship is lukewarm and I will not honor a lukewarm relationship. So many will be surprised when they face ME and discover that dancing with the world and also spending a little time with ME will keep them out of MY Kingdom. There will be many surprised.

Revelation 3:16. So then because thou art lukewarm, and neither cold nor hot, I will spue thee out of MY Mouth.

What do I want and expect from MY children? I want their life. I want it all in complete surrender. A dance with the world and a dance with ME is evil. Read MY Word. O' so many read MY Book and they take from it what they want so they can placate themselves, so they can enjoy the world and still feel that they can enter MY Kingdom when their life ends. What a shock to those who discover that I only receive those who have given ME their all - sacrificed their all. Their pursuit of wealth, fame, possessions was all in vain and ultimately keeps them outside MY Kingdom. Their own will and future planning has led them on a path outside of MY Will and apart from MY True Plans for their life - a life I created. The life I gave them and sustain.

O' yes no one lives and breathes from day to day except I ordain it. This is why MY children should not be so sure of their own selfish planning apart from MY Will and true intensions for their life. I can take any life I choose at Will. No one lives outside MY Decisions for their life. I give, I take as I see fit, as I desire. This is why it is pure foolishness when men create their own plans and make their own way apart from MY Will for their life. It is the height of pride and foolishness and it is evil. It is the way of MY enemy to lead MY sheep astray down paths of destruction by what looks so normal and right. It is the enemy's deceptive plan to deceive many.

Job 12:10. In WHOSE Hand is the soul of every living thing, and the breath of all mankind.

Psalms 104:29. THOU hidest THY Face, they are troubled: THOU takest away their breath; they die, and return to their dust.

CHAPTER 3

TRAINING IN HUMILITY

Daughter I am ready to give you Words. Listen closely as I speak. Now I want to go over new information. I want to talk about training in the way of being humble.

This is the way of the humble. A quiet, still heart are MY humble ones. They walk quietly never looking for position or privilege. They seek ME in all ways. They are ever-seeking their GOD. They do not want to be center-focus. They do not want to seek attention for themselves or recognition.

They only desire to be loved and cared for by ME, their GOD. They trust ME and I care for them. I meet their expectations. I deliver their needs. I bring them all the things they require to live by. I am their Rock.

I am ever faithful to MY humble servants. I bring them peace and calm in every storm. I am always at their side, ever abiding, always willing to serve them. I Love MY humble servants. They are a beautiful fragrance to ME. I Love them and they love ME. WE are inseparable. I am their AIR. They shine bright as stars. They do not seek the ways of the world. I keep them content. The world holds no sway over them. They seek ME for contentment and I bring them what they desire.

They are never disappointed. Very few walk this path. Very few find it. The ones, who do, find the road to MY Kingdom everlasting.

1 Peter 5:6. Humble yourselves therefore under the Mighty Hand of GOD, that HE may exalt you in due time: My humble servants always listen for MY Voice. They move when I ask them to and they serve when I need them to with a glad heart. They love to serve in MY Kingdom. They are content serving their KING and I bring them joy and peace.

MY Love flows over them. They never lack.

To be humble, you must consider yourself in last place, never needing first place.

It is wisdom to be last not first. The fools seek first place. MY humble servants are wise and know what pleases ME, their GOD. MY children are the humble, the ones the world never notices or sees, hidden away out of the view of the worldly.

They are of no account in this world, but in MY Kingdom, they are the rulers and reigners. They are exalted in MY Heavenly Realm. I honor MY humble ones. They sit with ME on MY Heavenly Throne and enjoy MY Presence. The humble who make themselves last in this life enjoy position in MY Kingdom. They are lifted up and held in esteem for their life of submission on earth. These ones bring ME joy and I give them peace, everlasting peace.

Mark 10:31. But many that are first shall be last; and the last first.

I walk with the humble and make MYSELF known to them. This is MY Gift for their sacrifice. What a sweet smell their love for ME is and I will honor them.

Humble is the way of the Kingdom of GOD. Everyone in MY Kingdom is filled with humility. Pride cannot enter in. It has no place in MY Kingdom, only peaceful submission to ME, GOD. This is MY Kingdom, full of quiet humility where everyone is satisfied with the love and beauty that overflows. There is no one who is dissatisfied with their life in heaven. Only hope and peace abounds. This world overflows with love.

1 John 2:16. For all that is in the world, the lust of the flesh, and lust of the eyes, and the pride of life is not of the FATHER, but is of the world.

CHAPTER 4

TRUSTING IN GOD

Let US begin MY daughter (February 7, 2012). Today MY child WE are going to cover new ground: I want to talk about trusting in GOD. MY children do not trust ME. They say that they trust, but their hearts are far from ME. They trust in themselves. This is evil.

They trust in the world and the things of the world.

They do not walk MY Path because they do not trust it. If they trusted ME, they would walk in MY Path, MY Will, MY Perfect Ways.

They seek other directions to go in. They move in other directions. They seek the world for all their answers through money, fame, possessions, security, romance, entertainment... everything, but ME, their GOD! They are living a lie when they say they trust ME and they seek answers from the world. Lies, it is all lies. "Trust in GOD," they say but then they never surrender their lives over to ME wholly and they continue to cling to the world for their answers, they live a lie and they don't even see it.

Yes, I bless MY children with abundance. I make it rain and shine on the righteous and the wicked alike. But MY children cannot say they trust ME and still continue to commit adultery against ME with the world. This is an abomination. I desire children who lay down their lives before ME in complete surrender and put all their trust in ME laying aside their future plans and trusting in MY Perfect Will for their lives. They do not need to strive and struggle and worry about tomorrow if they are in MY Will. Can I not care for the sparrow? How much more do I care for MY children who give ME their all and sincerely trust ME?

Matthew 5:44-45. But I say unto you, Love your enemies, bless them that curse you, do good to them that hate you, and pray for them which despitefully use you, and persecute you; That ye may be the children of your FATHER which is in heaven: for HE maketh

HIS sun to rise on the evil and on the good, and sendeth rain on the just and on the unjust.

Psalm 4:5. Offer the sacrifice of righteousness, and put your trust in the LORD.

I am a GOD WHO can be trusted. There is no other Rock. All else is sinking sand.

I am the GOD of the ages: ALPHA and OMEGA, BEGINNING and END. I can be trusted. Why waste time and worry on your own plans? No one even knows what the next hour will hold. Your plans can blow away in a single moment. Why do you cling to them so as if they will save you, as if they are reliable? It is idol worship for sure!

Matthew 7:26. And every one that heareth these sayings of mine, and doeth them not, shall be likened unto a foolish man, which built his house upon the sand.

Stop clinging to your imperfect plans. Give ME your life in full surrender. Only I know the future, your future. Only I know what you will be doing tomorrow.

Your own hopes and dreams outside of MY Will for your life will lead you to destruction because only those in MY Will by full surrender are safe, truly safe. All others are walking apart from MY Will in their own rebellious will and therefore cannot move forward in safety or security. This is serious, MY children.

Awaken and stop trusting in your own rebellious ways and trust in your GOD.

Only I know the way to the narrow path. Don't be misled thinking you can find this path apart from ME…that is foolishness. Few find this path because few stop clinging to their own ways. They think their ways are best because everyone around them is following this way, but the road to hell is broad. Don't trust the many around you who are misled. Can you not see this? What do you not understand about this, MY children?

Matthew 7:13-14. Enter ye in at the strait gate: for wide is the gate, and broad is the way, that leadeth to destruction, and many there be which go in thereat: Because strait is the gate, and narrow is the way, which leadeth unto life, and few there that find it.

So trust ME. I can be trusted. MY Words never fail. Read MY Book. I deliver those who truly want to be delivered. I am a GOD WHO delivers those who submit to ME in humility and brokenness. So come and be delivered and learn to trust your GOD.

CHAPTER 5

FORGIVENESS

Let US begin again (February 7, 2012). Now I want to talk about "forgiveness." Children, I want to speak to you about this matter of forgiveness. MY children are unforgiving in their hearts storing up grievances against each other. I cannot forgive those who don't forgive. Is this clear? How can I forgive you, if you, yourself cannot forgive those around you? Does not MY Word speak of this? Forgiveness is love. Unforgiveness leads to all kinds of sin: bitterness, revenge, wrongful judging, and on and on... It gives a foothold to the enemy to come in and destroy you. This keeps you from closeness, intimacy with ME, your GOD, and keeps you from receiving MY SPIRIT. This is serious.

Matthew 6:14. For if ye forgive men their trespasses, your heavenly FATHER will also forgive you. But if ye forgive not men their trespasses, neither will your FATHER forgive your trespasses.

If you are unforgiving, you cannot be ready for MY Soon Return. This will hold you back. It separates US.

Leave this unforgiveness behind. Forgive each other. Lay down your anger toward each other. What do you gain when you harbor anger toward someone else? You suffer more than the person you are angry with, can you not see this? Is your eternal salvation worth harboring anger toward another?

Mark 11:25. And when ye stand praying, forgive, if ye have ought against any: that your FATHER also which is in heaven may forgive you your trespasses.

You must search your heart and ask this question. What is worth losing your eternal soul over... a petty dispute? Forgive and walk away and feel a dark cloud lift. Even if the other person won't forgive you, pray for them, yes pray for your enemies. Pray for them with a sincere heart and I will warm your heart to those who harm you. I will give you a heart of flesh.

How can you expect those who do not walk in MY Way and those who do not possess MY HOLY SPIRIT to treat you as if they do? You must render patience, kindness, longsuffering to those who do not know ME. It is impossible for those who do not know ME, truly know ME, to behave as if they do. Can you not see this? You cannot expect this from those who walk apart from ME.

Matthew 5:44-45. But I say unto you, Love your enemies, bless them that curse you, do good to them that hate you, and pray for them which despitefully use you, and persecute you; That ye may be the children of your FATHER which is in heaven: for HE maketh HIS sun to rise on the evil and on the good, and sendeth rain on the just and on the unjust.

The world thinks it can run apart from its GOD. It fools itself. Only I hold everything together. Only I bring the right way to live, to men. This world, that shuns ME, lives under false direction and evil deception. It all has become so evil.

There is no truth, only compromise and deceit. Apart from MY Perfect Ways, mankind lives under deception and corruption. Nothing or no one can be trusted.

Only MY bride, who remains in the earth and walks in MY Perfect Will, is on the straight path. Only she is stable and true. All others walk the unreliable path of evil—unstable in all its ways.

Soon the bride will be removed and the world will lose all its light. Darkness will be all consuming. This day approaches.

Forgiveness: the key to making your way back to ME. Forgive everyone. There is no unforgiveness worth losing your very soul for...

Luke 6:37. Judge not, and ye shall not be judged: condemn not, and ye shall not be condemned: forgive, and ye shall be forgiven: Daughter, this is your LORD Speaking. Let US begin: Now I want to offer instruction in living with others.

Too many have disregard for each other - little patience, little respect. This is all leading to strife. It leads to discontent, hurt feelings. MY children are selfish. They want to be first in all things. They are very insensitive to the needs of others; they fall short in caring for others. This leads to arguments, anger.

Children I am saddened by this, but the crux of the problem stems from self- centeredness. This comes from a lack of humility.

Proverbs 15:33. The fear of the LORD is the instruction of wisdom; and before honour is humility.

Only from a humble heart will you be able to live among each other successfully.

You must lay down your desires and give so those around you remain content.

This requires taking a back seat to all those around you. This is the way of the humble. This produces fruit: peace, contentment, pleasant environment.

Few learn to live like this. Few find this Truth. But it is the way of peace, MY Way.

I give these rules for life so that MY children can live in peace and contentment, yet they choose their own way and ultimately have strife and much discontent.

When will they learn MY Road is the best Road to travel? I know everything. I know how MY children can best live together. I give rules and precepts to guide MY children into homes of peaceful dwelling and contentment. This, of course, requires that MY children lay down their ways and desires and follow MY Rules.

Psalms 34:14. Depart from evil, and do good; seek peace, and pursue it.

Selfish choices lead to unhappy homes. Let ME Rule over your home... let ME Reign in your hearts. MY Way is Calm, Peace, Love.

I will bring your home into the happy dwelling I meant for MY children. Submit your hearts to ME willingly and I will rain down tranquility.

Your household will exude quiet assurance, love, and peaceful living. Walk in paths of quiet contentment, humility, and caring for others' feelings bring fruit of satisfaction. Let ME rule over your household and I will deliver a home of gladness and joy.

Psalms 37:11. But the meek shall inherit the earth; and shall delight themselves in the abundance of peace.

CHAPTER 6

LIVE IN THE WORLD, BUT DO NOT BE "OF THE WORLD"

Let US begin. Today, I want to talk about living in the world. MY children live in the world, but do not need to be "of the world." The world is an enmity to ME. I am disgusted with its overwhelming evil.

Children you can walk among those of the world without partaking of the things of the world. The world will lead you down paths of destruction and heartache.

James 4:4. Ye adulterers and adulteresses know ye not that the friendship of the world is enmity with GOD? Whosoever therefore will be a friend of the world is an enemy of GOD.

I am your only source of wholeness, peace, and calm. Do not turn to the world for direction. You will only be misled. You must turn to ME for direction. Cling to ME in this vital hour. I hold all your answers.

I want to spare you sadness and grief, but you must turn your life over to ME in completion - only then can I take it and deliver you.

You can walk safely in the world and not be affected by its lures but you need ME to walk by your side. I can lead you through the endless distractions the world puts out to lead you astray and pull you away from ME.

I want you to focus on ME. Keep your eyes fixed on ME, your SAVIOR. I am your door to safety. All other doors lead to destruction. Don't be deceived and take your eyes off of ME. I offer hope in a world that offers none.

O' it appears to be hopeful, but what looks normal is deceiving.

Psalms 25:15. Mine eyes are ever toward the LORD; for HE shall pluck my feet out of the net.

These are the last hours. The world is in the end times. The world seems so convincingly normal, but all is not so - it is leading to the path of destruction.

Soon many will find this out too late. Open your eyes. The world offers only false hope.

Let ME Lead you. Surrender your life to ME. I will open your eyes with MY HOLY SPIRIT and you will be renewed and see things the way they really are and then you will see the Truth. Only MY HOLY SPIRIT can open your spiritual eyes that so deceive you about the ways of the world. I am ready to give you the spiritual eye salve to help this transformation take place. You have but to ask ME for it.

Surrender your life, heart, soul, spirit, and let ME give you the sight you need to navigate safely through the world...

Revelation 3:18. I counsel thee to buy of me gold tried in fire, that thou mayest be rich; and white raiment, that thou mayest be clothed, and that the shame of thy nakedness do not appear; and anoint thine eyes with eyesalve, that thou mayest see.

CHAPTER 7

RAPTURE AND MARRIAGE SUPPER OF THE LAMB

Let US begin. These Words are for whoever will receive them: Today I am going to talk about the coming rapture, the removal of the bride, MY church.

This moment arrives quickly. Many children are not ready. They fight ME and cling to the world. They want to walk in the ways of the world. They rush to and fro and pay no heed to the warnings I am giving... Soon the warnings will be done and I must come and the bride will be removed. She will be taken out of the picture.

Daniel 12:4. But thou, O Daniel, shut up the words, and seal the book, even to the time of the end: many shall run to and fro, and knowledge shall be increased.

Her identity is unknown to the world. She is well hidden. I have her cloistered away in safe keeping. MY Light shines through her—the last remaining light on earth. Time is short and soon this light will go out. MY sent ones will leave to their heavenly home safe from the tyranny on earth.

This rapture event will be a large event, the removal of MY ready children. No such event will ever be like it in human history. There will never be anything like it before or after. It is the greatest "Exodus" of all time.

MY children will depart in a moment and receive new glorified bodies. These bodies will be resilient and eternal. They will follow after the pattern of the glorified body I possess. I am the FIRST FRUIT of many others. These children will experience a life they have never known before, a glorious life, life everlasting.

1 Corinthians 15:51-54. 51Behold, I shew you a mystery; We shall not all sleep, but we shall be changed, 52In a moment, in the twinkling of an eye, at the last trump: for the trumpet shall sound, and the dead shall be raised incorruptible, and we shall be changed.

For this corruptible must put on incorruption, and this mortal must put on immorality. So when this corruptible shall have put on incorruption, and this mortal shall have put on immorality, then shall be brought to pass the saying that is written, Death is swallowed up in victory.

There will be many wonderful things ahead for MY raptured children. Let ME give you a peek: When MY children arrive, they will be greeted by their loved ones: family and friends already in the heavenlies. I will be looking on. This is a moment of great glory. What a gift to be reunited with family long missed... Then MY children will be ushered to the great Marriage Supper of the LAMB. I will preside over this event.

Revelation 19:9. And he saith unto me, Write, Blessed are they which are called unto the Marriage Supper of the LAMB. And he saith unto me, These are the true sayings of GOD.

The table will be lavishly prepared: every accoutrement will be provided. The details of this event will be astounding. MY children will be seated in front of a place setting with their name lettered in pure gold. Each place setting will have golden utensils embedded with jewels. There will be solid gold plates also studded with jewels. The tablecloth will be of pure silk spun with golden threads.

Light will shine through the weave. The cups will be gold with jewels around the rim.

Each place setting will have a gift especially for each child. The gift will be a precious reminder of MY Relationship with this child. It will be unique for each child. Each gift will have special meaning to each child of OUR long lasting relationship. There will be many surprises at this Event - MY Marriage Supper.

Matthew 22:2. The Kingdom of Heaven is like unto a certain king, which made a marriage for his son, Each child will have an angel who waits on him. The food is prepared in MY Heavenly Kitchens. Nothing will be amiss. All food items will be of heavenly proportions, food from earth that is recognized and food from heaven never seen before. Beauty unspeakable will be this table setting.

MY Table will be full of light: candles of light, beautiful Menorahs. MY children will wear robes of light. They will exude light as there will be no shadows.

James 1:17. Every good gift and every perfect gift is from above, and cometh down from the FATHER of lights, with whom is no variableness, neither shadow of turning.

I will lead a toast to MY bride. I will sing her praises as she is most beautiful to ME. There will be dancing and music all around and making merry.

The bride will see ME in all MY Glory as I will be dazzling to the sight. MY beauty will shine through and MY Love will flow out and overwhelm all attending. MY FATHER will be looking on in great delight as there will be much dancing and making merry.

I will dance with MY bride and WE will be as ONE. MY children will dance and make merry. All hearts will be glad. No one will be sad. This will be a great hour of glory and love.

Doves will fill the air. They will fly in beautiful patterns and formations spelling out beautiful messages for MY bride. She will be in awe.

I will present MY bride with a ring. OUR Names will be written on this ring.

Flowers will be everywhere of all colors: new colors and old colors. Fragrance will fill the air, beautiful fragrances. MY children will be lost in the ecstasy of it all.

Luke 15:22. But the father said to his servants, Bring forth the best robe, and put it on him; and put a ring on his hand, and shoes on his feet: MY angels will fill the skies with dancing, singing, and music-making. Heavenly instruments will play beautiful music. The stars will cry out celebrating the LAMB and HIS bride.

Job 38:6-7. 6Whereupon are the foundations thereof fastened? Or who laid the corner stone thereof; 7When the morning stars sang together, and all the sons of GOD shouted for joy? All the heavenly hosts will gather and sing praises over the LAMB's Great Nuptials.

Everyone will sing praise to the KING, HIS bride cometh. She has made herself ready. Let the joy begin!

Revelation 19:7. Let us be glad and rejoice, and give honour to HIM, for the Marriage of the LAMB is come, and HIS wife hath made herself ready.

The LAMB WHO taketh away the sin of the world unites with HIS beloved in Holy Matrimony. Great is HIS Name! Praise His Holy Name among all the heavenlies for HE is betrothed to HIS beloved and HE has won her heart!

John 1:29. The next day John seeth JESUS coming unto him, and saith, Behold the LAMB of GOD, which taketh away the sin of the world.

MY children will also be shown their mansions: O' daughter the beauty, the splendor.

Eye has not seen or ear has not heard what waits MY glorious bride who loves ME.

1 Corinthians 2:9. But as it is written, Eye hath not seen, nor ear heard, neither have entered into the heart of man, the things which GOD hath prepared for them that love HIM.

Daughter, these mansions will be more delightful than anything earth has to offer. Nothing can compare to the magnificence of what MY bride has in store for her. These homes will suit the taste and interests of each child. No two mansions are alike. Each one is different from the other.

John 14:2-3. In MY FATHER's House are many mansions: if it were not so, I would have told you. I go to prepare a place for you. And if I go and prepare a place for you, I will come again, and receive you unto MYSELF; that where I am, there ye may be also.

MY children will be flabbergasted at what they will discover in each mansion. All have details that will delight and enthrall its owner. There is nothing on earth to describe the ornamentation and beauty of each of these incredible homes.

All the interiors have unique surprises. These mansions are living. They take MY children to and from wonderful places for MY children to enjoy and experience.

WE will share in these adventures together. WE will laugh and explore. The excitement will never end. There will be gardens and pleasures all throughout.

Music will fill the air and lovely fragrances. Each home will be filled with love and laughter. Loneliness will never be a problem in heaven. I am always with MY children making merry and enjoying each other's company.

Psalms 36:8. They shall be abundantly satisfied with the fatness of THY House; and THOU shalt make them drink of the river of THY Pleasures.

MY Love will surround their every move. Laughter, love, and joy are the rewards of these eternal homes, joy unspeakable, everlasting delight.

This is only a taste of the things to come. MY children do not have any comprehension of what awaits them. There is no way to accurately paint a picture of what awaits with what exists on earth. Only witnessing it in person will give its true description.

So MY children come and enjoy heavenly delights in the everlasting Kingdom with homes especially prepared with loving care for MY bride.

Psalms 16:11. THOU wilt shew me the path of life: in THY Presence is fullness of joy; at THY Right Hand there are pleasures for evermore.

CHAPTER 8

PREPARE FOR THE RAPTURE

Let US begin. Now daughter, the coming days before the rapture there is much to prepare. MY children need to spend time with ME in the secret place, quiet time, time to get to know ME. I need their attention and company. I want to share MY Heart with them. I need a complete, full surrender of their hearts, lives, and attachments of the world.

Psalms 91:1. He that dwelleth in the secret place of the Most HIGH shall abide under the shadow of the ALMIGHTY.

MY children are attached to the world. They believe this world holds everything for them. This world is empty and cold-hearted. Each man for himself, no one really cares for anyone else. It has become a dog eat dog world. Everyone is after what they can get from someone else for their own selfish purposes. It is a world of hopelessness and misery. And MY children still yet cling to it believing that it still holds a bright future for them. They are mesmerized by the lost who promote their lost ways.

MY children need to pull away from this nonsense and come back to the Living GOD, their MAKER, WHO holds all the answers to this life and the next.

I am the Great GOD of all living and breathing spirits. I possess the keys to life everlasting. Surrender to ME your all before I make MY Great Entry to the earth, collect MY bride, step aside, and allow the earth to receive its just due.

Job 12:10. In whose hand is the soul of every living thing, and the breath of all mankind.

This is about to take place. Surrender is required to be among MY bride, MY rescued children. There is no exception. Surrender in full allows MY SPIRIT to come into your spirit and to renew it and clean your heart with the covering of MY Blood Ransom and the enlightenment provided through MY Word. This is all necessary to deliver your soul, to be cleansed spotless, wrinkle free, made white, and ready for your removal to safe keeping. If you doubt this, read MY Word!

Ephesians 5:25-27. 25Husbands, love your wives, even as CHRIST also loved the church, and gave HIMSELF for it; 26That HE might sanctify and cleanse it with the washing of water by the word, 27That HE might present it to HIMSELF a glorious church, not having spot, or wrinkle, or any such thing; but that it should be holy and without blemish.

Pray for this HOLY SPIRIT filling. Lay down your life, repent of your sin. Begin fasting in show of your remorse for sin carried on before ME, your HOLY GOD! I will replenish you; I will lead you to everlasting Truth in MY Ways and MY Will.

Your will will lead you to destruction. It is the broad road MY Word speaks of - come into MY Will. It is the narrow path, the safe path. I will take you to it.

Matthew 7:13-14. 13Enter ye in at the strait gate: for wide is the gate, and broad is the way, that leadeth to destruction, and many there be which go in thereat: 14Because strait is the gate, and narrow is the way, which leadeth unto life, and few there be that find it.

MY Word will guide you to the path of Light. All other paths lead to everlasting destruction. Come into MY Light, MY Will. Give ME your life. Let ME relieve you of past sin and show you the road that leads you to freedom from the bondage of sin.

Psalms 119:105. THY Word is a lamp unto my feet, and a light unto my path.

No matter what, sin keeps you in bondage to it. I can free you, but you must first surrender, repent, and admit you have sin you want to be freed from and do it from a repentant, sincere heart. I will delight in freeing you of this sin bondage that ties and binds you. No matter what holds you prisoner, I can free you.

Nothing is impossible for ME - nothing! I came to set the captives free! You have but to ask!

Luke 1:37. For with GOD nothing shall be impossible.

Let ME free you of this weight. Let me lift your sorrow and grief. Let ME ease your mind and take your burden. Let ME prepare you for MY Coming Glory! All this is yours—surrender; put away all your earthly desires and come to ME in full surrender. I will give you peace that passes all understanding and you can be made right before MY Face. I can bring you into right standing with ME, the FATHER, and the HOLY SPIRIT.

Philippians 4:7. And the peace of GOD, which passeth all understanding, shall keep your hearts and minds through.

This love cannot be bought or purchased. It is free - free for the taking - free for the asking. Hurry though as it has a limited time offer as time is growing closer for MY Return. Don't delay. The hour is now to wash in MY Blood and prepare.

1 John 1:7. But if we walk in the light, as HE is in the light, we have fellowship with one another, and the Blood of JESUS CHRIST HIS SON cleanseth us from all sin.

Let US begin, daughter. Today I want to discuss the hour for those left behind.

The hour after the rapture, the world will not be the same. There will great upheavals everywhere. The world will not look the same. Terror will strike the land. MY lukewarm children will know what has happened and fear; great fear will strike their hearts.

The world will not function normally. The landscape will not even look the same.

There will be fires and calamity everywhere. The people will be defenseless as mobs of people will be looking around for people to prey on and rob from.

There will be no forces out to help the people as everything will be in chaos.

Many will lose their lives as sudden destruction comes to earth. Whole parts of the world will not look the same again as many people will perish at once.

1 Thessalonians 5:3. For when they shall say, Peace and safety; then sudden destruction cometh upon them, as travail upon a woman with child; and they shall not escape.

Panic will set in from all corners of the earth. There will be nowhere to turn for relief. The food will diminish to nothing. There will be desperation everywhere.

This will go on for a period of time until the antichrist steps in and brings the world under his control.

At first, it will seem as relief to the people who are frantic to see a form of normal again, but the relief he is bringing will bring death to many. Those who refuse to fold into his system will be executed and many even tortured and tormented.

Refusing to be part of his system will not be pleasant as he will have no tolerance for anyone. He is evil to the core. He will bring the whole earth under his tyranny. All lands will bend to his control out of desperation to find relief from the chaos left from the rapture.

This will be the darkest day known to mankind. Many will kill themselves looking for relief. This is not MY Solution so it is not to be considered as one.

The antichrist will instill the mark of the beast on the people as a means of control. Refusing the mark will bring a sentence of death. There will be no exceptions.

Revelation 13:16-17. And he causeth all, both small and great, rich and poor, free and bond, to receive a mark in their right hand, or in their foreheads: And that no man might buy or sell, save he that had the mark, or the name of the beast, or the number of his name.

Revelation 14:11. And the smoke of their torment ascendeth up for ever and ever; and they have no rest day or night, who worship the beast and his image, and whosoever receiveth the mark of his name.

Many of MY lukewarm followers will then understand the price they must pay to come into MY Kingdom. So many will not surrender to the antichrist and so many will die for their faith. It will be a large number.

It will not matter how many die to the antichrist. His lust for power and control will rule over his heart. He will have no concern over the many who lose their lives. It will be a dark day for those who profess MY Name. My Name will bring a death warrant to many. MY Name will be opposed and represent rebellion to the antichrist system and they will want to eradicate all who promote ME and MY Ways.

What a dark hour approaches children. These have been dark hours on earth in the past but never as dark as what lies ahead. This will not be a pleasant place for anyone carrying children. Darkness will reign. This is what MY lukewarm church will face.

Lukewarm churches will come back to ME in large numbers. People will seek ME like never before. I will of course be there but they will still have to go through hard times. Families will be separated and sadness will ensue. All this because MY children have hardened their hearts and remained stiff necked to MY many warnings. All this could be avoided, if MY children would come to ME, cry out in humble-hearted repentance, seek MY Face, learn to know ME in intimacy. Run into MY Waiting Arms. I will show them the Truth about the hour of MY Soon Return and how to be prepared as the bride.

Come children. Run, I am waiting to save you from all of this. I am the Great RESCUER. MY Desire is to save you. No one needs to be left behind. There is room for all who come and lay their life down before ME. I require surrender of your total being and repentance for your sins. Don't be fooled as there is no other way. Let ME bring you relief from this coming hour! Let US begin again. MY children believe that they have many years into the future. They do not understand that I have lost MY Tolerance with this world.

MY children are too caught up in the world to see how far removed the world is from MY Truth and what I, GOD represent. Even their churches are far from MY Words, MY Truth, MY Book.

The leaders of MY flocks are caught up in worldly activities and they do MY Work to please themselves. They no longer have or pursue a pure love for ME. They pursue wealth, fame, credibility from those around them and believe I will bless them.

They believe large numbers in their churches equate success and that I am pleased. I am only pleased if MY leaders point their children to seeking ME first in all their ways and to walk with ME in quiet intimacy. Very few are teaching this because it does not tickle the ears of the many they want to draw into their buildings. Many bring money and money makes everyone happy, but MY Kingdom is not about riches in this life.

Luke 16:13. No servant can serve two masters: for either he will hate the one, and love the other; or else he will hold to the one, and despise the other. Ye cannot serve GOD and mammon.

MY leaders are far from ME and why not? If they appease large numbers then when is their time for ME? I am the reason they exist! I am the ONE WHO brings the sun and the rain.

This is a dark hour and it grows darker each day, yet MY leaders cloak this Truth from MY flocks. They hide it and only bring Words of happiness and joy. MY flocks are deceived and are not being prepared. They think all is well and they continue on as always.

What words of warning would revive them? What must they hear to believe MY Book has laid out all the Truth before them, yet no one hears, no one believes.

What must be said for the church to take hold of the warnings and put aside their obsessions with the things of the world and watch and prepare?

Hosea 4:6. My people are destroyed for lack of knowledge: because thou has rejected knowledge, I will also reject thee, that thou shall be no priest to ME: seeing thou hast forgotten the law of thy GOD, I will also forget thy children.

They are soft and being misled. Time is getting away and the church remains grossly complacent as if everything is alright. How deluded the lukewarm church is. How lackluster its pursuit for ME is and all I represent. If the church really pursued ME in intimacy, then none of MY Warnings would come to them as a surprise and they would be whole-heartedly heeded.

This is a great hour of darkness for the churches. Very few are sitting up and taking notice. Very few are walking in MY Precepts and Ways. Grace is not extended to those who willfully live rebelliously, unrepentantly. You can quench and grieve MY HOLY SPIRIT and then what do you do O' church?

Ephesians 4:30. And grieve not the HOLY SPIRIT of GOD, whereby ye are sealed unto the day of redemption.

When you drive MY SPIRIT out of your beautiful buildings because HE is too extreme for your taste—I and MY SPIRIT are ONE. Who are you worshipping if you have excused MY SPIRIT and the move of MY SPIRIT from your presence? Just who are you worshipping? You are idol worshipping!

Acts 7:51. Ye stiff necked and uncircumcised in heart and ears, ye do always resist the HOLY GHOST: as your fathers did, so do ye.

You have created a god of your own making, a god who suits your worldly likes and desires, but it is not the ONE True Living GOD. It is merely an idol. You think the people in the past who worshipped golden statues were scandalous - you are no different! Come to ME in humble repentance churches and I will cleanse your souls. I will forgive you for your pursuit of mammon and for getting away from ME. I long to bring you back to MYSELF. Let ME revive you and bring you peace and make you right with your GOD.

Mark 8:36. For what shall it profit a man, if he shall gain the whole world, and lose his own soul? As it stands, you are far from ME and MY Ways. This I will not bless. Please turn back to ME O' lost church! I am still waiting yet a little longer. Delay is not an option. Stand alert and heed this warning. Take action! Many lives are at stake!

2 Timothy 4:3-4. For the time will come when they will not endure sound doctrine: but after their own lusts shall they heap to themselves teachers, having itching ears. And they shall turn away their ears from the truth, and shall be turned unto fables.

CHAPTER 9

ABOUT THE LOST CHURCH

Let US begin. This Word, I want to talk about MY lost church, those who believe they are secure in ME but are far from ME. I am addressing you now: Many are in churches they believe are giving them the full Truth about ME and what I stand for - but the Truth is there are watered down versions of what I stand for in most of the churches around the world. This means they are carrying half truths to the people because the people will not tolerate the whole truth.

They do not want to know MY Full Gospel. They want to hear what tickles their ears and placates their desires to be in the world and live worldly lives.

The hour is coming for MY Return and I cannot take MY half-hearted, lukewarm believers. They will be left behind. They will know then what their semi- interested faith has done for them.

Revelation 3:15-16. I know thy works, that thou art neither cold nor hot: I would thou wert cold or hot. So then because thou art lukewarm, and neither cold nor hot, I will spue thee out of MY Mouth.

Now children, you cannot rely on your church leaders to present you with all the Truth. You must seek ME yourself for all the Truth. You must read MY Book, surrender to ME whole-heartedly and ask to be filled with MY SPIRIT from a repentant, humble heart. There is no other way. I want a full commitment. I will exchange your life with a life that is full and abundant and you and your eyes will be opened to Truth, MY Truth. Then you will understand what I require to be received into MY Kingdom.

MY church has lost sight to what it means to be MY follower. They do not follow MY Precepts and Ways. They look for loopholes to do exactly what they want and still feel good about themselves. This has been going on now for a very long time but now it is rampant and very few want the whole Truth, very few want to understand what MY Word really says. They want little stories that make them feel good as they come and go but never really want to know ME or WHO I am.

They only think they know ME. I am not truly known by most of MY followers.

Most only dabble in a relationship with ME. They do not fully understand what it means to make ME their GOD. I am just a bystander looking in on their life, never really taking part in their life, never really sharing an intimate relationship.

Matthew 7:21-23. Not everyone that saith unto me, LORD, LORD, shall enter into the kingdom of heaven; but he that doeth the will of MY FATHER which is in heaven. Many will say to me in that day, LORD, LORD, have we not prophesied in THY Name? And in THY Name have cast out devils? And in THY Name done many wonderful works? And then will I profess unto them, I never knew you: depart from ME, ye that work iniquity.

This saddens ME greatly as this is the true reason I created MY children, for intimacy with ME, to walk this life's path together. Yet the world so entices them that they have chosen the inferior way than to come and know their MAKER.

How sad to be so intrigued with the creation and to reject the CREATOR; MAKER of all they are intrigued with. How very sad indeed! MY children, you do not see that I require holiness and fidelity.

Children, I want to be your FIRST THOUGHT, your FIRST LOVE, your FIRST - ALL in all. This is why you were created—to be MY companion eternal. If you choose not to walk this road with ME now, how can I expect WE can be eternal companions? Who do you expect to be eternally tied to...ME or MY enemy? You need to ask yourself this question.

MY Love is deeper than any love man knows. Do not sell yourself short seeking inferior satisfaction. You will never know a greater love than MINE.

Children, you need to search your heart and examine your soul. Where do WE stand, you and I? Where do I fit in your life? Am I on the outside looking in or do WE really have a relationship? Am I the core of your life? Where do you want ME to be? You must ask yourself.

I wait on you. MY Arms are wide open to bring you into a full fledge relationship with your MAKER, your GOD.

The hour approaches for important decisions to be made. Do you want to be among MY bride? She is MY all in all. She waits on ME and watches for ME. I am more than a fleeting fancy for her. I am not someone she calls on intermittently or when she is in need of something. She and I are interlocked. I move, she moves. WE blend, WE are ONE. She is in MY Will and she moves down MY Narrow Path. OUR Course is aligned.

So MY children, I leave the choice to you. Although I want you to choose for ME, you still have a free will. So I invite you to come into the Perfect Relationship and Purpose you were designed for. The choice is yours. Don't wait too long to choose. The offer will not last forever.

CHAPTER 10

LUST FOR THE WORLD

Yes daughter, WE can begin. Susan, this is what I want to talk about today: The sin that rises up in the hearts of men - it is the sin of lust for the world. All the ways of the world are evil, evil men inspiring evil acts. All that the world does is apart from GOD.

The world is not in MY Will, so it is not of MY Will. The world often professes to know ME, but it is far from ME and MY Truth. It runs full force in the direction that it willfully wants to go in without ever consulting ME, its MAKER. This is evil.

To run outside of MY Will is evil. The only will that is not evil is MY Will. Do you not see this MY children? How can this world move in the direction of GOD now when it has gotten so far from WHO I am and what I stand for? I stand for holiness, purity of heart, law and order, truth and morality. This world challenges all MY Ways and doesn't even come close to what MY Book sets out as Truth and MY Everlasting Way.

The world maligns ME and MY Ways every chance it gets and those who follow ME. MY Ways are not respected or revered. If they were, this world would not experience the woes, hardships, disease, and sadness that overwhelms it. MY Way brings blessings. The world's way brings cursings and cursings abound.

Only those who really walk close to MY Word and ME receive the peace and calm that I deliver even in the worst circumstances. This is MY bride who follows ME without flinching. She knows ME. She loves ME. She does not get far from ME.

She knows I am her life source, her power, her love, her strength.

Where else can she go to receive this comfort? She knows better than to leave MY Side for other lovers. I have been tried, tested, and true to her. I am her ALL in all. No one can take MY Place in her eyes.

The world does not know MY Love. It has settled for an inferior version of satisfaction. How sad for those who follow after the world and its ways, believing this world system holds all the answers.

Soon, this world will lose its last remaining light when I remove MY bride from its midst. Once she is out of the picture, the world will then be a very dark, desolate place. There will be nothing to look for that resembles a guiding light of Truth and Beauty, only gross ugliness and evil will ensue. This is the world soon-coming.

This is what is about to take place.

2 Thessalonians 2:3-4. Let no man deceive you by any means: for that day shall not come, except there come a falling away first, and that man of sin be revealed, the son of perdition; who opposeth and exalteth himself above all that is called GOD, or that is worshipped; so that he as GOD sitteth in the temple of GOD, shewing himself that he is GOD.

2 Thessalonians 2:6-7. And now ye know what withholdeth that he might be revealed in his time. For the mystery of iniquity doth already work: only he who now letteth will let, until he be taken out of the way.

A world that does not live by MY Laws and Precepts is like a ship without a rudder. This is a ship that is dead and dying, a sinking ship.

Soon children, you will see death and destruction like never before. Because this world has chosen to turn away from its GOD, its CREATOR. Don't be fooled.

The world cannot continue to exist apart from MY Truth and MY Ways. She is a sinking ship. It is time to get off this ship. Are you coming when I call out MY faithful ones? Will you come after ME or will you stay behind clinging to the false hope that this world holds all your answers? Are you still listening to wolves in sheep's clothing that nothing is wrong and all is well? These wolves who do not really know ME, who have a form of godliness but deny the power thereof? Are you going to continue to be misled and blinded because you enjoy the world too much?

2 Timothy 3:5. Having a form of godliness, but denying the power thereof: from such turn away.

Come partake of GOD and discover there is a Greater Truth, there is a Greater Peace, there is a Greater Love. I am HE! Chase after ME, children! Get to know ME. I am worth pursuing. I am worth knowing, devoting time to. I am the ONE WHO brought you into being. Do you not want to spend eternity with ME? There is an alternative. It is a place that all the good of this life that comes from ME is missing. Yes, all that is good in this world comes from ME. I Created it all. Without ME, none of the good things that you enjoy so and take for granted, that spring from the Heart of GOD, will you ever experience again.

So give this some serious thought. You decide: your eternity with or without GOD. You choose, you decide. Am I taking you when I come to rescue MY bride? This is your choice. But there are prices to be paid. You must step away from your love and pursuit of the world because the world's way is not MY Way. I will let you come to a decision about the direction you choose. Very few are choosing MY Way, very few...

1 John 2:15. Love not the world, neither the things that are in the world. If any man loves the world, the love of the FATHER is not in him.

CHAPTER 11

THE WORLD IS HEADING FOR TROUBLE

Let US begin, MY daughter. Now I want to talk about the events about to take place.

The world is heading for trouble. There are great dark clouds growing all around.

Soon, very soon, this world will change. All of it will change overnight once the bride is removed.

The world will be become dark as it's ever been with no hope of recovery. Soon MY children, this will take place. Begin to prepare for this reality. I am not an exaggerator of Truth. MY Words can be trusted. The hour of these changes are coming now swiftly. The course has been laid out and it cannot be stopped.

The world has become wicked and no man, government, or power can stop what is coming. This is the unfolding of Revelations and the last days. The hour of MY SON's Return arises. Soon the world will know what has transpired like a thief in the night. There is no stopping this event. It has been foretold and it is now coming to pass, just as MY Words said it would.

1 Thessalonians 5:2. For yourselves know perfectly that the day of the LORD so cometh as a thief in the night.

Children, you need to make preparations. Make yourselves ready. Be ready for MY Soon Coming and MY SON's Approach. HE Comes with HIS angel armies riding across the sky to retrieve HIS beloved. This hour is nearly here.

Arise O' faithful ones. Make ready. Prepare for the Greatest Event in all history, the BRIDEGROOM Coming for HIS bride. Come and make ready. All must be prepared. Come and be readied by the Blood of the LAMB. Cover yourselves in HIS Blood. It is available.

Surrender to HIS Great Love. Make HIM your BEGINNING and END. WE are ONE: FATHER, SON, and HOLY SPIRIT.

Now children, the enemy is making his plans. He is preparing to launch his attack against humanity. All civilization is about to change to be completely undone. I do not want you to be caught unaware. But this great upheaval is about to take place. You need to make yourselves ready. Humanity is about to decline into a state of irreparable madness and evil. Only when MY SON Returns to earth will all of it come to a close - only then will the evil be vanquished.

2 Thessalonians 2:8. And then shall that Wicked be revealed, whom the LORD shall consume with the SPIRIT of HIS Mouth, and shall destroy with the brightness of HIS coming: Soon children, you must come to a conclusion: What will you believe? What will you hold onto: A vanishing earth or MY Will and MY Ways? I offer an Everlasting Kingdom. Don't believe this earth holds any future for you. All is about to fold up very soon. The landscape will forever change. Don't be greedy, clinging to a future that doesn't exist. You are wasting your time.

Come to terms with this Truth and wake up to it. I am giving you Truth. Read MY Book and match it to what is unfolding now. The similarities are seamless because it is all coming to pass just as I said it would so long ago. This is not coincidence. This is the Mighty Word of GOD coming to pass.

MY Word does not falter or fail. MY Words are solid. I am GOD ALMIGHTY, EVERPRESENT TRUTH, UNRELENTING, ALL POWERFUL, UNCHANGING KING of Kings, LORD of Lords. MY Words are unchanging...

1 Peter 1:24-25. For all flesh is as grass, and all the glory of man as the flower of grass. The grass withereth, and flower thereof falleth away: But the Word of the LORD endureth for ever. And this is the Word which by the gospel is preached unto you.

51

Come awake O' you sleepers. Now is the hour to awaken. Be alert. Now is the time. Remove your blinders. Put down the things of the world and pay attention.

Midnight approaches.

Children, I implore you. Don't be caught off guard. Be ready. Make ready.

The hour of the SON's Return is at hand...

CHAPTER 12

MY SOON COMING

Let US begin. Now daughter, today I want to address concerns of the world regarding MY Soon Coming.

The world is about to experience an explosion of change. Change is coming from all sides: the swift removal of MY bride - those who have made themselves ready: purified themselves in MY Blood and through the washing of MY Word. Also the dramatic result of the removal of the bride followed by sudden destruction and the rise of the antichrist system.

Ephesians 5:25-27. 25Husbands, love your wives, even as CHRIST also loved the church, and gave HIMSELF for it; 26That HE might sanctify and cleanse it with the washing of water by the word, 27That HE might present it to HIMSELF a glorious church, not having spot, or wrinkle, or any such thing; but that it should be holy and without blemish.

This will be overnight cataclysmic change. Nothing will ever be greater, than this change, in world history. Those left will feel it and those taken will know it.

Many will die during this change as destruction is coming to this earth. There will be continual destruction as MY Wrath will be poured out. What the earth has witnessed so far is only a foretaste of what is coming. This is why I continue to pour out MY Warnings through these signs and MY many servants: young and old alike.

MY Warnings have been clear and consistent, both through MY Word and through the warnings I give through others. I do not shift or change - I am EVERLASTING TRUTH. MY Truth does not change - MY Word does not change.

Children, as this hour closes in, the time has come to be vocal and to warn those around you of the pending doom coming to the earth.

So many think MY Book is a fable or great tale, but every Word is Truth and it is all coming to pass.

Soon, Revelation will play out in clock work order. You will see it all come together before your very eyes. It already is if you would just take time to read and notice. Everything that is happening was foretold so long ago. So put your doubting aside. Stop listening to others who do not know ME. Read MY Book for yourself. Seek MY HOLY SPIRIT for guidance. HE is always available to reveal Truth, to render eye salve - what you need to see this Truth.

Revelation 3:18. I counsel thee to buy of me gold tried in fire, that thou mayest be rich; and white raiment, that thou mayest be clothed, and that the shame of thy nakedness do not appear; and anoint thine eyes with eyesalve, that thou mayest see.

I do not want you to be caught unaware. I want you to wake to the Truth and to be ready and sober. I want MY children to come into the Light and see the Truth.

Truth is available, readily available. There is no reason now to remain in the dark and not be ready for what is coming. I can guide you, lead you. Let ME do it, I long to do it.

I long to hold you and assure you that you can avoid the troubles coming to the earth, all is not lost. Children, come into MY Faithful Arms. I am a Caring, Loving GOD ready to care for you, no matter what you have done or where you have been. Come, Come! This is the hour of your rescue. Don't get caught into a world spiraling out of control because it rejects the ONE True Living GOD and MY Perfect Ways.

Many will wait too long and regret their decisions. Don't let this happen to you.

I am ready to share MY Heart with you... open up to you... bring you into MYSELF and share intimate moments. This is MY Longing: to uplift you and bring you through difficult circumstances.

Please let ME share with you in life's most difficult moments. I want you to let ME comfort you. I long for this relationship with you - O' how I long for it. Don't push ME, your MAKER, away. Embrace MY Offer to be close to you, closer than anyone has ever been to you. That is what I Offer MY children, a relationship that is unlike any other human relationship—one with your GOD WHO knows you better than any other... I Offer this closeness. I bring you MY Heart. It is MINE to give and I give it to you. It is yours for the asking. So few ask for it, but it is available.

Children, I lay open MY Heart, invite you to come in, partake, enjoy MY Presence.

Come to know ME as more than just a distant, far off GOD.

I can be approached. I can share your deepest thoughts and concerns with you. I can comfort you, take you through the worst times, and encourage you during your most difficult moments. I am a Loving GOD, willing to be open and share intimacy with you, to walk this life together. You never have to walk this road alone again. I am always at your side. I am there to comfort, support, and encourage. Come to know ME in the relationship I always meant for US to share together.

This is why you were created - to be intimate with ME. That is your purpose in this life. You may believe otherwise, but I am your MAKER and I say it is so. I want to be there for your lows and your highs, for the hard times and the glad times: sharing life together, walking the straight path together. This is the life I had planned for you: MY Perfect Plan and Will for your life.

Psalms 139:3. THOU compassest my path and my lying down, and art acquainted with all my ways.

So come to ME. Surrender your life to ME. Lay it before ME in humble submission, and I will take it and clean you up and make you ready for MY Kingdom and you may partake of MY Marriage Supper as MY bride. You have but to ask and I will give you all this: I long to bring you into MY World.

I, GOD am ready and waiting. Stop living your life apart from your MAKER.

CHAPTER 13

THE HOUR HASTENS, MY CHILDREN

So Let US Begin. Children, I am addressing MY Children: The hour hastens MY children. I come swiftly on wings of white doves, on a gallant steed flanked by millions and millions of angels. This day approaches. You need to be ready, waiting, watching, looking for ME.

2 Thessalonians 3:5. And the LORD direct your hearts into the Love of GOD, and into the patient waiting for CHRIST.

I am razor sharp, always on time. MY Word is Good. I do what I say and I do it on time.

This hour is coming to a close. So do not become discouraged for those who await ME with great expectancy, for you will not be disappointed.

I am a GOD WHO Delivers on HIS Word. MY Word is good, solid, I am the ROCK! No one who places his faith in ME will be disappointed—No one! I change not. I am the same yesterday, today, and forever. I am the ALPHA and the OMEGA! Children, you must prepare. Put aside your worldly cares and make preparation.

How do you prepare? I want humble submission.

I want lowly, sincere repentance and your acknowledgement of your sin before a HOLY GOD you are accountable to.

I want full surrender - leaving nothing out.

I want you to put all your faith in ME.

I want you to fill yourself with MY HOLY SPIRIT. Come and receive a full oil lamp.

I want you to wash yourself in MY Word I want you to clean yourself in MY Precious Blood—Blood I gave for your ransom.

I want you to seek ME in all your ways and to get to know ME in the secret place.

I want you to walk with ME day by day, leaning on ME every moment.

I want you to pray to ME and talk to ME all through the day.

This is your LORD Speaking. Children, I want you to be alert, bright-eyed and watching for ME. I want you to see the signs, know the times, and read MY Book.

Don't be in the dark about the Truth.

This is a dark hour and it will not get brighter. There is not brightness coming for this world, only horror, sheer horror awaits it.

Listen closely: MY Truth is always reliable. You can always depend on it. I have said this hour of darkness was coming and here it is now upon you. Children, this is not the time to be complacent, caught sleeping. Arise, come to MY Truth.

Make your amends with ME. I am waiting on you. Release your grip on the world. That you believe so whole-heartedly in. Don't cling to a crumbling world as if it holds all the answers for you. Stop waffling between the world and ME. I cannot receive your half-hearted commitment. This will never be accepted. You must come to ME in full submission or WE can never be together for eternity.

These are MY requirements to come into MY Kingdom. This is what MY bride is ready to do to be part of MY World completely. She is ready to give ME her all in all. I want complete submission. Nothing less will do.

Children, I died for you a complete and humbling death - nothing was left undone. There were no loose ends - I took it all: ALL of ME - that is what I gave.

Never did I walk from MY Desire to receive your due punishment. I received it in full measure. Every moment was grueling and torturous. I was like a LAMB to the dogs. Nothing of ME was left when it was over. The price was paid in full.

Psalms 22:16. For dogs have compassed ME: the assembly of the wicked have enclosed ME: they pierced MY Hands and MY Feet.

Do not reject this great price I paid for your penalties. If you reject this offer you will not receive another remission for your sins. There is no other remission for sins. Although people look for it—it does not exist. I am the only payment: MY Spilt Blood, MY Suffering on the Cross, MY Broken Body, MY Broken Heart. I paid your price, your penalty, and I did it freely of MY OWN Will so that you could enjoy fellowship in full with MY FATHER, I, and MY SPIRIT. This is what I endured and why.

Hebrews 13:12. Wherefore JESUS also, that HE might sanctify the people with HIS Own Blood, suffered without the gate.

This is a Precious Gift, MY children. Price cannot be put on it - no price would suffice. Don't count it worthless or trivialize it. Treat this gift with respect. There is no greater gift than this one afforded you by your GOD.

Now children, I do not ask for payment for this gift. There is no payment you could make that could even touch its value. It is free - given freely and available for your taking. Do not shun or reject such an Enormous Gift from such a Humble and Generous GOD.

Rejecting such a Great Gift will bring eternal penalties. To reject such a Gift will bring eternal hell. Do you understand MY children? So do not handle this Gift lightly. Care for it because it is a Most Precious Offering by your GOD for your salvation and everlasting freedom from hell damnation.

Hebrews 10:29. Of how much sorer punishment, suppose ye, shall he be thought worthy, who hath trodden underfoot the SON of GOD, and hath counted the Blood of the covenant, wherewith he was sanctified, an unholy thing, and hath done despite unto the SPIRIT of grace? This is a Rare Gift indeed. So few in this world look upon it and value it. So few will walk MY Streets of Gold, because of their cavalier attitude toward MY Great and Gracious Gift to mankind. Do not be fooled. To mishandle such a Great Gift is very dangerous. So hold it close, cherish, and revere MY Gift and be glad for it because through it is eternal salvation, hope, and life everlasting in the Great Kingdom of GOD.

MY Gift to mankind only I could have paid and only I accomplished what no other living soul could have achieved. I give freely MY Love undone, MY Love, Greater than any other known love.

Come sup with ME at MY Table of Love and experience love like no other. I give freely. This is a once in a lifetime offer. Take...take freely. It won't always be available.

This is MY Love Offering Poured Out. Come whosoever will...

LORD YAHUSHUA

MIGHTY KING

HUMBLE LAMB

OFFERING POURED OUT.

CHAPTER 14

THE WORLD HAS TURNED AGAINST ME

Let US begin, MY child. Children, I want to address the world that has turned against ME: This world has turned against ME and the things I stand for. It has become gross and uninhabitable.

James 4:4. Ye adulterers and adulteresses know ye not that the friendship of the world is enmity with GOD? Whosoever therefore will be a friend of the world is an enemy of GOD.

MY children, this world is filled with sin. There is nowhere to turn for holiness and truth. Even MY churches are distant from ME. Even those who claim to know ME are distant. They keep ME at arm's length. I am not even consulted by MY OWN leaders. They seek ME not. They do not know ME. Their churches have become dens of iniquity because they preach false messages. They neither know ME nor care to know ME. I am an unknown GOD.

The world has no time for its GOD. It reaches out to ME only in speech but not in Truth. This world is full of liars and thieves, men who are boasters and idolaters pursuing the world and the ways of the world, but never its GOD.

How sad for those who do not know ME, but say they do and think they do. I am a GOD WHO can be known. I am not hidden to those who pursue ME. I am not unknown to those who come close to ME in humble submission. I am known.

Draw near to ME and I will draw near to you.

Psalms 73:28. But it is good for me to draw near to GOD: I have put my trust in the LORD GOD, that I may declare all THY Works.

Children everywhere you turn, evil lurks. There is nothing in the world that isn't prepared by the enemy to throw you off the track to being close to ME, GOD.

The world system is set up to derail MY children and to keep them apart from ME.

If MY enemy can keep you occupied with lesser gods and idols then you cannot seek ME and find your true path to MY Salvation, MY Sanctification, and MY Freedom.

This is the enemy's plan to see you fail, to cause you to miss MY Rescue, and to lose your place in MY Kingdom. This world system is tied to the plans of MY enemy. Everything is oriented to self-seeking and self-fulfillment and not GOD- seeking, GOD-pursuing, GOD-finding. He does not want you to come looking for ME. He wants you to be locked into a system that teaches "self" is most important, rely on "self," plan your own future, trust no one but yourself.

This is not MY Way children. MY Way, MY Will says follow after GOD, rely on GOD, seek GOD's Will, GOD's Way.

When you seek your own will, plans, you are outside MY Will and that is sin. You are living in sin if you are outside MY Will.

How can you know MY Will for your life if you do not seek after ME and surrender your all to ME? You must lay down your own plans, your own ways, and allow me to direct your life. Only by walking in MY Will for your life can you really experience freedom and peace, the peace I give.

Following your own way apart from ME, will lead to destruction. You will never be able to break free from sin. MY Will is the fullness of the HOLY SPIRIT and having a full lamp. This is the only way to be ready for MY Soon Coming, to be saved and rescued.

Children, you must awaken. This is Truth! There is no other Truth!

Matthew 25:4. But the wise took oil in their vessels with their lamps.

CHAPTER 15

LEADERS DO NOT FOLLOW ME

Let US begin, again. MY children, I am agonizing over this world that holds me in such little esteem.

I am not held in high regard at all. I am very seldom called on by MY OWN people - those who lead MY flocks. They make their own plans completely apart from ME. I cannot rely on them. They do not tell their people the Truth, only what they believe they want them to hear.

There is nowhere for MY people to go for Truth. They must come to ME! They will be misled in their own churches. They will be confused by what looks normal and right, only falling into divisive traps laid for them by MY enemy.

He wants them to believe they can rely on the words of their leaders and that seeking ME apart from that is not necessary. Only Truth can be found by the regular washing of MY Word. This requires discipline. MY children, you are MY disciples and discipleship requires discipline. If you are too caught up in the distractions of the world, how can you hope to be in MY Will children? This cannot be. I am not a GOD WHO can be disrespected or disowned.

This world is beginning to see the affects of disowning its GOD. There are consequences to walking away from GOD, grave consequences. I do not take kindly to those who come close to ME and then seek the world as what they believe is a better alternative to ME. This is not a wise thing to do at all. Yet, this is what the world is doing: abandoning any hope by serving itself and seeking its own ways.

The hour has come for MY Soon Return. Where are you at MY children? Are you with ME or are you drifting away from ME back to the world? The world offers you no hope. It is a failing, crumbling, lost world, lost because it no longer seeks GOD for its answers.

Demons are now ruling the world through all types of means: through the messages you receive; through the world system that is in place; through churches that are misled.

Only MY Word can be relied upon - it is unchanging. Focus on MY Word. Dig deep in its pages. Find time to read MY Words. Spend time with it. Pray for MY SPIRIT to reveal all Truth to you. He will, if you ask HIM sincerely. He longs to lead you to Truth. This is HIS Greatest Desire for you to be led to Truth and cleaned up by MY Word.

1 Corinthians 2:13. Which things also speak not in the words which man's wisdom teacheth, but which the HOLY GHOST teacheth: comparing Spiritual things with Spiritual.

Children, do not let this world pull the wool over your eyes. Do not allow the enemy to lead you astray as so many are led. Be alert. Come into MY Light. Be fed by MY Truth with MY Holy Hand. I long to feed you with Truth: to nourish you with the teachings from MY Word. Let ME bring you into MY Light. Let ME show you what you have never understood before. I have many things to share with you. I want to pull you out of darkness.

This is the time for the Truth to be known and not watered down truth or half- hearted truths and lies. You do not want to take a risk with your own salvation.

So come to ME. Cry out for Truth. I will give you Truth, unchanging Truth.

Now children, now is the hour.

I am YAHUSHUA, MAKER of All.

CHAPTER 16

THE HOUR OF MY RETURN APPROACHES

Let US begin, daughter. The hour, MY children, is coming for MY Return. This hour approaches as sure as night turns into day. I am coming and there is no stopping this event.

You must consider the importance of this event. It will have ramifications for everyone: Not a living, breathing soul will not be affected in some way on earth.

There will be those escaping with ME to bliss and those facing utter destruction and tremendous loss.

The way you face this event is your choice - how will you experience this event will be your decision. Will you come away with ME when I bring MY bride out to safety or will you choose to stay behind and face the worst: MY Wrath poured out and MY enemy in full force? Now this seems like such a simple choice - but few are choosing to come out with ME to safety. Few are looking for ME or believing that the time for MY Coming is nigh. Why do you think this is MY children? It is because sin has got the best of them. They have become too adapted and accustomed to this sin-filled world, loving its ways and wanting to partake in it too readily. They do not read and trust MY Word. They do not search ME out for MY Answers. The world and men hold more weight in their minds.

Children, I cannot save those who won't turn to ME in humble, childlike submission. Without full surrender to ME, I cannot rescue you when it comes time to for ME to remove MY church. She will be taken and you will be left. Then MY children who are left will have to contend with MY enemy. It will be a great hour of darkness. Relief will not be found.

Mark 10:15. Verily I say unto you, Whosoever shall not receive the Kingdom of GOD as a little child, he shall not enter therein.

Still you have an opportunity to come back to ME in the closing days before MY Soon Coming. If you surrender yourself to ME, submit your will to ME, and I will make you into a new person and prepare you for MY Kingdom.

I see very few willing to make these steps, only a portion of the population is truly seeking ME on a level of intimacy that I require. Few are entrusting their lives over to ME. Most are trusting their lives to the world and the skewed thinking of men.

Children you must come to your senses. I am the only ONE WHO can help you.

There is nowhere else to turn. Yes, you can turn to the world, but it is now in a hopeless condition, escalating downward daily.

You must come alive. Come to ME. Don't be fooled by what now looks normal.

Looks can be deceiving. The world cannot go on apart from ME. I am the MORAL COMPASS - without ME and MY Unfailing Ways, this world cannot be sustained with compromised morals.

MY children soon, very soon all this will happen: MY Soon Coming. I do not want you to be lost or left. I want you to come to ME. This is MY Invitation to you. I want you to come along side ME. Walk the Narrow Pathway with ME. Let ME Guide you. Let ME Lead you... take MY hand.

Don't miss the great chance to become the bride. She is beautiful and prepared.

I love her dearly. She is MY sweet church who loves ME above all else. She bears witness of ME. I am her "ALL in all." I am coming to save her from the horrors to come. She will be spared all of what is coming, swept away in MY Waiting Arms.

CHAPTER 17

ABOUT THE ANTICHRIST

Let US begin. Children, I want to address something new today: I want to talk about the antichrist and his rule and reign on earth.

Soon he will be coming into the earth to rule and reign - all will change.

The earth has never known such a tyrant as this. He will keep no prisoners. He will be bent on destruction. Anyone who stands in his way will know destruction.

It will be a most dark and bleak time.

1 John 2:22. Who is a liar but he that denieth that JESUS is the CHRIST? He is the antichrist, that denieth the FATHER and the SON.

Those who speak MY Name out will be found in contempt. MY Name will mean death. Many of MY Own will cower in fear to use MY Name. This will happen worldwide. It will be worldwide terror, destruction widespread. The world has never known such destruction.

Revelation 20:4. And I saw thrones, and they sat upon them, and judgment was given unto them: and I saw the souls of them that were beheaded for the Witness of JESUS, and for the Word of GOD, and which had not worshipped the beast, neither his image, neither had received his mark upon foreheads, or in their hands; and they lived and reigned with CHRIST a thousand years.

The antichrist will come at a time when the world is looking for answers and solutions to the wake of destruction left following the rapture of MY bride. This event is rising soon. The world is going to know trouble like it has never known before.

1 John 4:3. And every spirit that confesseth not that JESUS CHRIST is come in the flesh is not of GOD: and this is that spirit of

antichrist, whereof ye have heard that it should come; and even now already is it in the world.

The antichrist will try to eliminate all who stand for MY Ways, MY Testimony. The antichrist will bring about the mark of the beast as the first order of business to control the people.

Those who don't buckle under his demands to take the mark will be eliminated as dissidents against the system. Those who take the mark will ridicule and persecute those who refuse the mark. It will be a most dark hour. Those who willingly take the mark will be forever lost. It is ownership of the antichrist system.

Revelation 14:11. And the smoke of their torment ascendeth up for ever and ever: and they have no rest day or night, who worship the beast and his image, and whosoever receiveth the mark of his name.

Children you must think clearly about your desire to ignore these warnings and what is coming over the earth in short order.

The hour approaches for MY Coming for the bride: those who will be rescued - MY true church. This hour is hastening and coming nearer as the antichrist system is about to come into effect.

The antichrist will be ruthless and blood thirsty. He will allow nothing to get in his way. His is full of anger and lust for power. People matter to him not. He has no compassion at all - he only lives to see himself rule and reign over the earth.

He will be bent on destruction to bring his forces into power. Nothing will stop him until I come back to earth to put a stop to it all. This is when, and only when, he will be stopped. There will be no stopping him otherwise. No human, no organization can stop him. He will be unrelenting in his evil.

2 Thessalonians 2:8. And then shall that Wicked be revealed, whom the LORD shall consume with the SPIRIT of HIS Mouth, and shall destroy with the brightness of HIS Coming: There are evil times

rising. Behind the scenes, the plans are being laid out for this system to come into play. The way is being made clear for the rise of this evil.

Soon the population who remains after the church is raptured will realize the antichrist system of destruction and control that they are being ruled by.

The lukewarm, left behind Christians will then fully comprehend what has taken place before their eyes. The regrets will be enormous. Many will fall away from the pressure of the antichrist. The way of the antichrist will seem too easy compared to not following it. It will truly be an hour of hard decisions. Many will know in their hearts what they must do and by courage and desire to see MY Kingdom will follow through with the difficult decisions they must make. Their faith will carry them: faith in rejecting the antichrist system as the right decision and choosing for ME, GOD. Many will not have this kind of faith and courage. It will be a dark hour.

Revelation 19:20. And the beast was taken, and with him the false prophet that wrought miracles before him, with which he deceived them that had received the mark of the beast, and them that worshipped his image. These both were cast alive into a lake of fire burning with brimstone.

Truly children, you want to become sober quickly and prepare yourself to be rescued—to be prepared to be made ready.

This hour is closing in. You need to be ready... waiting ... watching... looking and eyes fixed and ready for ME. I am the only DOOR - I am the EXIT - I am the ESCAPE! I will soon be holding the door open and then it will shut. This will be the one and only escape to what is coming. This is coming. The hour approaches.

MY church needs to make ready.

Matthew 25:10. And while they went to buy, the bridegroom came; and they that were ready went in with him to the marriage: and the door was shut.

The antichrist is in the wings. He is making preparations to rise to power. He is looking for earthly domination. He will stop at nothing. Terror is his moniker. He will reign in terror and no one on earth can stop him. His power comes through MY enemy. This is the one truly behind the terror.

Do not downplay this reality. Nothing looks as it truly is. Things look relatively normal, but looks are deceiving. And this is devised by MY enemy. He wants to throw you off course. He doesn't want you to walk the straight and narrow path toward ME and MY Soon Rescue.

Deception is running high now. Too many are deluded into thinking all is well. All is not well children! All is not well! The world is coming apart at the seams, flying apart.

Children open your eyes wide. Come to terms with what is about to happen.

Come awake, look around. Dig deep into MY Word then look at what is going on in the world.

This world is rejecting its GOD on all four corners unilaterally. I can no longer tolerate it. I am lifting MY Hand of Protection over the earth and allowing it to have its desire, a world without its GOD, its MAKER, CREATOR.

I am a Reasonable GOD, but when the world asks ME to step aside, I will do just that. Then you can find out what things look like without MY Protection! I am a Patient GOD, but MY Patience has run out for these people who reject ME so! Children, I am pleading... please come to your senses! Come to ME in surrender.

Give ME your life. I will accept it. I will cover you in MY Precious Blood. I will clean you up in MY Word. The hour approaches. You need to be cleaned up so that you can come with ME up hither when I call out MY bride to follow after ME to safety. You can still come. Prepare yourself though, make ready quickly. This hour waits on no one. Nothing will stop MY Return.

I am YAHUSHUA...GREAT KING...HUMBLE GOD.

John 15:3. Now ye are clean through the Word which I have spoken unto you.

CHAPTER 18

THE TIME APPROACHES FOR MY SOON DESCENT

Let US begin again. Now it is time for ME to talk about a new topic: Children, the hour approaches for the time of MY Soon Descent. This comes quickly. Many, so many are not ready, so many are falling away... so many have never been ready. There are many changes about to take place in the world. I want you to come to terms with this Truth.

Children, the hour approaches of MY Soon Return, I see that very many are not ready. Many believe they are ready but are not. Many are still cavorting with the world. This cannot be, MY children. You must break your ties with the world.

She is a sinking ship and she will take you down with her.

MY children, I do not value the time you spend apart from ME chasing the things of the world. You seek answers through the world. It cannot be MY children.

You are looking at empty hope... empty promises... and empty truth. Your loss will be great if you continue down this empty rabbit hole. It is leading to disaster.

Why do you persist in believing that the world holds any truth for you apart from MY Truth? I AM TRUTH!

1 John 2:15. Love not the world, neither the things that are in the world. If any man loves the world, the love of the FATHER is not in him.

Children, listen closely, your time is running out. You have little time to pull yourself together. It is now time to prepare. If you plan to come with ME, you must focus on MY Coming. MY enemy is preparing to make his move very soon.

His plans will only be altered some by MY Coming.

Do you not see, MY children that you should be wide-eyed and ready for the events that are about to take place? Soon, no one will not be affected by the changes coming over the earth. Either you are coming with ME out to safety or you will stay and deal with MY enemy and the wrath to come.

This day is coming, MY children. It is coming and no one can stop it. You need to make yourselves ready as the hour is nearing. It is coming swiftly.

Come to know ME. There is no other way. If you don't make time to get to know ME, you cannot come out with ME to safety.

You must surrender your all to ME. I am waiting on you, children. Who will come to ME in full surrender? Who will come to know ME, really know ME? This is what I require.

I made a way for you. I have prepared a way. I have paid a large price for your ransom unto freedom so that you might be able to join ME when I come for MY bride. She is ready and I am coming for her.

The price I paid was huge. No one else could have done what I did. Only I could have accomplished what I did. Only I could have paid such a great price - GOD WHO comes to the level of being crushed for mankind. This price cannot be calculated. No value can be placed on such an act. There is no amount that would ever cover the price that was paid.

Isaiah 52:14. As many were astonished at THEE; HIS Visage was so marred more than any man, and HIS Form more than the sons of men: Children, do not reject such a Gift. Come, I give it freely to you. Please consider this offer. It waits for you to take it and become free, free to come out with ME when I pull MY children to freedom.

It is all yours - you must come and surrender. Give ME your all in all. This is what I ask of you. If you do not make yourselves MINE, you are still MY enemy's. You are not your own. You either belong to ME or MY enemy. Choose to be MINE. I await your answer.

This is your LORD and SAVIOR, YAHUSHUA, GREAT MESSIAH.

CHAPTER 19

MAKE PREPARATIONS

Let US begin (February 19, 2012). Children, I have many Words: The hour approaches for MY Return. You need to make preparations. I want to take you with ME when I come for MY beautiful bride, but if you are not ready, I cannot take you.

You must make yourself ready. Show ME you are ready. I need you to be watching for ME. I need all eyes to be fixed on ME. If you are not watching, you cannot be ready. Only those watching will be ready.

Hebrews 9:28. So CHRIST was once offered to bear the sins of many; and unto them that look for HIM shall HE appear the second time without sin unto salvation.

Some say they don't need to watch to be ready. This is a lie from the enemy. He is crafty and filled with deceit. He wants to lead all MY children astray and off the narrow path. You must stay ready at all times. You must be watching and ready for you do not know the hour I cometh. I will come as a thief in the night. Does MY Word not say this? MY Word is clear about this. Many will be taken aback, unprepared, and caught off guard because they failed to watch and stand ready.

Do not be among this group who refuses to heed MY Warnings to watch and remain ready. This group will be saddened and devastated to discover they have been left behind to face the worst: human upheaval and earthly disaster.

Don't be reticent and nonresponsive to MY many warnings. Be ready… come alive… awaken!

2 Timothy 4:8. Henceforth there is laid up for me a crown of righteousness, which the LORD, the Righteous JUDGE, shall give me at that day: and not to me only, but unto all them also that love HIS Appearing.

MY children, you even allow your ministry work to stand in the way of being ready for this most important event. Many churches and many of MY leaders will be left. Don't get caught in this trap. Be on guard. Be prepared. Be wary.

Don't let your house be burgled. Don't stand by and let your house be broken into. The watchman who isn't prepared is caught off guard when the thief comes unexpectedly –safeguard yourself, make ready. As you don't know the hour I come to snatch MY church away.

Matthew 24:42-44. Watch therefore: for ye know not what hour your LORD doth come. But know this, that if the goodman of the house had known in what watch the thief would come, he would have watched, and would not have suffered his house be broken up. Therefore be ye also ready: for in such an hour as ye think not the SON of man cometh.

Once I come and take MY church, MY bride, I will not return that way again. The door will be shut and no man will be able to open it.

Luke 13:24-25. Strive to enter in at the strait gate: for many, I say unto you, will seek to enter in, and shall not be able. When once the master of the house is risen up, and hath shut to the door, and ye begin to stand without, and to knock at the door, saying, LORD, LORD, open unto us; and HE shall answer and say unto you, I know you not whence ye are: MY Coming is sure and swift. I will not delay this event for anyone or anything. It is coming, surely it is coming. Tomorrow may be too late, that is how close MY Coming is. Do not delay in your decision-making, and in making preparations for MY Soon Return. Wait too long and you will miss ME.

Now is not the time to be loafing and wondering off in the ways of the worldly.

Children, do not tarry in your decision-making for ME. I will not wait forever on MY lukewarm church to awaken.

Please consider these Words seriously. I am not going to hold back forever waiting on a church who refuses to embrace ME and look for ME. This cannot be.

MY Plans will go forth and I will take MY ready ones: those who seek ME diligently and expectantly. Those are the ones who I will take out with ME - all others will be left.

I am sorry if these Words seem harsh, but MY Warnings have been clear and consistent. Why do people believe I will not follow through on MY Words and MY, O' so many, warnings? Have I, GOD not been consistent eternally? I changeth not.

Hebrews 13:8. JESUS CHRIST the same yesterday, and to day, and for ever.

Be prepared, as I am ready to claim MY beloved. I am ready to get her. If you want to be among her, than make yourself ready. The hour is "now" to prepare.

Time is wasting. Watch and be ready.

These are MY Words. I am True to MY Words.

Your LORD, YAHUSHUA.

CHAPTER 20

YOUR TIME IS ALMOST UP

Let US begin (February 20, 2012). I am ready to give you Words: Children, it is I, your LORD and I am here to give you new directions.

The world is winnowing away quickly. The time is coming for the world to soon face MY Wrath. This hour is coming very quickly children, at a rapid pace. There is little time left on the clock. The world's troubles are closing in. Soon all will be aware of it, very soon.

Revelation 14:10. The same shall drink of the wine of the wrath of GOD, which is poured out without mixture into the cup of HIS indignation; and he shall be tormented with fire and brimstone in the presence of the holy angels, and in the presence of the LAMB: Children, you need to sit up and pay attention. Do not neglect, O' so important, warnings. Be vigilant in making preparations. MY Coming is close. There is little time to waste. You must awaken. I cannot wait forever on you, children. I cannot.

I must bring MY bride out and leave. She is ready. She has made herself ready. I want you to be ready also, MY children. Come to ME in humble submission. This is the hour of MY Soon Approach.

Don't wait forever. You do not have "forever." Your time is almost up.

I know this comes to you as a shock or hard to believe, but the truth is, time is nearing to a close before I remove MY bride. She is ready. I am ready and the world has turned its back to ME in unison.

Very soon, MY waiting bride will be waiting no longer and I will not allow her to stay behind to face what is soon coming to all those on earth who have turned against ME. She has made herself ready and the hour approaches for her evacuation into safekeeping.

Revelation 19:7. Let us be glad and rejoice, and give honour to HIM, for the Marriage of the LAMB is come, and HIS wife hath made herself ready.

This will be a grand event on a scale never known in the history of mankind ever before.

Children make preparations to come out with ME. Join ME in the air. I want to take you out with ME. I will keep you safe from what's coming. Soon, very soon, it is all approaching.

Don't be deceived by what looks normal and right. Too many will cling to the world, as if she holds all the answers. She holds only terror and grief very soon.

Do not be dismayed by these warnings. Embrace them as Truth.

Turn to MY Book. Study the Pages. Let Truth unfold before you, MY Truth.

Pursue ME, pursue MY SPIRIT. Let MY SPIRIT show you Truth. Allow HIM to come into your life and give you fresh, insightful understanding of MY Word. Men cannot show you the Truth, only MY SPIRIT.

1 Corinthians 2:11-14. For what man knoweth the things of a man, save the spirit of man which is in him? Even so the things of GOD knoweth no man, but the SPIRIT of GOD. Now we have received, not the spirit of the world, but the SPIRIT which is of GOD; that we might know the things that are freely given to us of GOD.

Which things also we speak, not in the words which man's wisdom teacheth, but which the HOLY GHOST teacheth; comparing Spiritual things with Spiritual.

But the natural man receiveth not the things of the SPIRIT of GOD: for they are foolishness unto him: neither can he know them, because they are Spiritually discerned.

Children, this hour is closing in. Let ME work on your heart. Let ME clean you up in MY Redemptive Blood. Let ME cover your sins with MY Perfect Blood Ransom paid in full by ME on the cross, the shameful cross, where I bled to death for your sin. I did this for you, MY children. All of you - I bled for all - all who would receive this Gift.

Philippians 2:8. And being found in fashion as a man, HE humbled HIMSELF, and became obedient unto death, even the death of a cross.

Yes it was MY Love and Willingness to save mankind from their wrongs under the cursings of this world. Now this Gift is yours if you choose to take it and receive a full pardon for your sinful ways.

You must want it though. You must come to ME in full submission. I want to see you walk away from your ties and love of the world. I cannot have you in MY Kingdom if you are still in love with this world.

So you have a choice to make: MY Ways or do you choose to go your own way with MY enemy? There is no middle ground - it is either one or the other: your will or MY Perfect Will for your life. This is the choice you must make.

If you come into MY Perfect Will, you must come to ME in humble submission and deep repentance for your sin. I will cover you in MY Blood and take away your sin past. All records will be destroyed and your life will be as new.

Hebrews 13:12. Wherefore JESUS also, that HE might sanctify the people with HIS Own Blood, suffered without the gate.

This is what awaits you if you come to ME in humble surrender and repentance over past sin. Now is the hour for this decision. Do not wait. This hour is coming for MY Return. No man can stop it.

You need to be ready. Make yourself ready. I wait on your answer.

This is your Patient, Loving GOD, YAHUSHUA

CHAPTER 21

APART FROM MY WILL,
YOU ARE RUNNING AGAINST ME

Let US begin, MY daughter. Children I want to speak to you about a new topic.

Very soon, MY children, I will arrive to remove MY church. So few are ready... waiting... watching, so few will be taken. This is serious, MY children, very serious.

Very few of MY children are really paying attention, so few even care. Many are not reading MY Book or practicing MY Words and following MY Rules that I have set before them. Many just do as they please with no care for what I think at all.

They are completely out of MY Will and making their own willful choices apart from ME. When you run apart from MY Will you are running against ME. This is sad children, that so many do not believe MY Word and choose to follow the world instead.

Children, the world is an enmity to ME. You cannot have the world and ME both.

James 4:4. Ye adulterers and adulteresses know ye not that the friendship of the world is enmity with GOD? Whosoever therefore will be a friend of the world is an enemy of GOD.

What does this mean to be part of the world? It means turning to the world for all your answers: following after the world for your future security, thinking it holds all the answers for you. This is false security - looking to men for answers - men who know nothing really about the future. Only I, GOD knows what the future holds. The world seeks after men and demons for answers. The world system is MY enemy's system. He wants to keep MY children distracted by all types of things so that they never seek ME for answers, so they never seek to know ME in a close, intimate way. This is dangerous, MY children.

Psalms 20:7. Some trust in chariots, and some in horses: but we will remember the Name of the LORD our GOD.

He wants you to stay far away from ME where he can entrap you and destroy you.

He will use all kinds of methods to entice you away. He will use your ministry work, your family, your pursuit of money and wealth, entertainment, and every distraction you can imagine. This is his strategy to get your attention away from ME and to keep it focused on everything else.

These are his plans to destroy you and he is successful with most people. Only a remnant truly follows closely after ME, pursues ME, and comes after ME. This is MY true church. These are MY true disciples, who lay down their life to follow ME.

Why do you persist in following after the world, when I am the ONE, True Perfect LIGHT? I am LIFE EVERLASTING. I give you life, I sustain you. I am the ONE WHO guards your life. I am the ONE WHO gives life and takes life - no other.

Job 12:10. In WHOSE Hand is the soul of every living thing, and the breath of all mankind.

Why do you persist in disregarding ME and pursuing other lovers, empty lovers? You are digging a hole for yourselves - one you won't be able to get out of.

Come to ME. Repent and surrender your whole life over to ME. Only I hold all the answers. Only I can make things right for you. Only I hold the key to your future. Get to know ME in an intimate way. Follow hard after ME and I will give you the key to the Kingdom. This world holds nothing for you, only hardship, disappointment, and soon death and destruction are coming to this earth.

Stop pinning your hopes on a dead and dying world - dead because it no longer acknowledges ME as LORD and MASTER by any government in the world.

All world leaders pursue other beliefs than ME as the undisputed LORD and CREATOR. This is an abomination and I will not take this lightly.

The world does not tremble in fear before ME, therefore I must soon re-educate them as to WHO I am. I am taking MY small remnant of true believers out to safety and then the world will realize I am a GOD to be reckoned with and not ONE to be disregarded. Soon then, I will lift MY Hand of Protection and MY enemy will be operating in full force upon the earth - he and his army of devils. It will be a dark time for the inhabitants of earth.

Psalms 111:10. The fear of the LORD is the beginning of wisdom: a good understanding have all they that do HIS commandments: HIS praise endureth for ever.

What can I do to get these Truths across to you? It is all written in MY Book, but very few desire to know the Truth. They run to and fro across the land seeking knowledge and wisdom, but never coming to the Truth.

Daniel 12:4. But thou, O' Daniel, shut up the words, and seal the book, even to the time of the end: many shall run to and fro, and knowledge shall be increased.

It is a sad hour for mankind: men who chase after the world but desire to have no knowledge of their own CREATOR. This is a sad time for mankind. And the effects of disregarding ME, GOD are obvious: rampant evil - crime, disease, death, economic disasters, wars, and rumors of wars. This is the trouble men bring on themselves when they walk away from their GOD and pursue the world.

Children, come back to ME. It is yet not too late. I will take you back. I am waiting on you. Run into MY Arms. Come and follow ME. WE can still be together for eternity. I can make you MY own. You can come into MY Kingdom and enjoy everlasting life with ME there.

Yes children, you can pursue ME, your MAKER or the world apart from ME. This is your choice to make. I am coming soon for those who choose ME as their ONE and ONLY LOVE apart from the world. Make your choice between ME and this world, because I must come soon to rescue MY own, those who choose against this world for ME, their GOD. What will you do? I am waiting patiently, but not for long. Soon I will have no choice but to remove the bride to safety.

This is your LORD and MASTER CREATOR of the world YAHUSHUA.

CHAPTER 22

EVIL IS COMING TO DESTROY THE WORLD

Let US begin again. Children, this is your FATHER Speaking. I have more Words to give out today.

There will be a large storm front coming over the world - it is called "evil." It is coming to destroy the world and those who inhabit the world.

It is coming after I remove MY bride to safety. She will come out first. She will not witness the horrors to come. The plague coming across the land will drive the people to madness. Horrors unspeakable will come over them. It will be an hour of pure terror.

Humans will be in desolation and panic. No one will be trusted, what an hour of horror awaits.

The antichrist will make the scene. He will come into full view and his powers will be of worldwide dominion. No one will be able to stop him. Past tyrannical leaders pale in comparison to his power, domination, and lust for blood. He will be unmatched in the terror he brings to the earth. No one will be able to hide.

There will be no relief, no escape from his tyrannical control.

There will be only one escape during his reign and rule: death and dying. This will be a dark time for human history.

Revelation 18:4-5. And I heard another voice from heaven, saying, Come out of her, MY people, that ye be not partakers of her sins, and that ye receive not of her plagues. For her sins have reached unto heaven, and GOD hath remembered her iniquities.

Children, waken to this Truth. Read MY Book. Read the description of what's to come. Don't be caught off guard. Bring yourself relief - come into MY Waiting Arms. I stand ready to save you. I am ready to receive you, to bless you, and bring you into MY Wonderful Kingdom, where there is everlasting love and beauty. I will bring you to MY Marriage Supper where WE will unite and share OUR Love forever more.

You don't need to fear the future. You don't have to worry about what tomorrow holds. You only have to surrender to ME. Make a full commitment to ME. Give ME your all: your life, your soul, your heart, your future plans. Make ME fully LORD and MASTER. I will guide you out to safety.

So few are coming, so few want to be part of MY Great Rescue Mission, when I bring MY children out to safety and carry them to MY Heavenlies.

You will receive a new glorified body. It will be a body full of light, MY Heavenly Light. It will be radiant, eternal, unchanging, glorious. MY children, MY bride will be beautiful, lovely to behold.

Yes, this transformation of MY church is about to take place. She will never look the same again. She will be spectacular. This transformation will take place in the twinkling of an eye. In one moment, MY church will be changed, ready for her BRIDEGROOM, made ready for MY Presence in ultimate purity and holiness: a spectacular sight.

1 Corinthians 15:51-54. 51Behold, I shew you a mystery; We shall not all sleep, but we shall be changed, 52In a moment, in the twinkling of an eye, at the last trump: for the trumpet shall sound, and the dead shall be raised incorruptible, and we shall be changed. For this corruptible must put on incorruption, and this mortal must put on immorality. So when this corruptible shall have put on incorruption, and this mortal shall have put on immorality, then shall be brought to pass the saying that is written, Death is swallowed up in victory.

She will be made beautiful in all her raiment. I know MY bride, I know that she watches ME and looks for ME. Her faith is unrelenting and consistent. She is the one I died for. She is the one who receives MY Gift, MY Free Gift to mankind for salvation. Very few actually want this Gift and pursue it. This makes ME sad, children. I bled and died a horrible death to save all men. Very few want this salvation. Very few take this salvation and commit to ME fully.

Come MY children, don't be among the ones left and lost. Come to your senses.

Pursue ME with both arms opened wide. Run into MY Waiting Arms.

This hour is collapsing quickly. You are about to see the beginning of the age of evil and great tribulation. Waken quickly. Fill your oil lamp. If it is not filled, you cannot come.

Matthew 25:4. But the wise took oil in their vessels with their lamps.

Come and receive MY HOLY SPIRIT in all HIS Fullness. HE will bring you into a full relationship with ME. I can then wash you in MY Blood and clean the stains off of your garment and make you ready for MY Kingdom. This is so you can be wrinkle- and spot-free: MY beautiful bride.

Ephesians 5:25-27. 25Husbands, love your wives, even as CHRIST also loved the church, and gave HIMSELF for it; 26That HE might sanctify and cleanse it with the washing of water by the Word, 27That HE might present it to HIMSELF a glorious church, not having spot, or wrinkle, or any such thing; but that it should be holy and without blemish.

I want to bring you to this place, this place of freedom and everlasting life. Just come to ME in full surrender and I can begin to make you ready. Time is wasting.

Make your choice. Are you staying behind or are you coming out to freedom and safety. Now children, decide. I want you to be ready, really ready.

MY Love Awaits You, Your KING, YAHUSHUA.

CHAPTER 23

THE CLOCK IS ABOUT TO STRIKE MIDNIGHT

Let US begin again. Children, this is your LORD Speaking. I have many Words to share.

The hour is late, MY children. It is running so late. The clock is running out. It is about to strike midnight. Two minutes left remaining on the clock.

This means you have little time left to prepare, I mean really prepare your hearts, to make yourselves ready. It is the hour to which MY Coming is bearing down, MY Coming to pull MY bride free from the tyranny and wrath to follow. She will not be caught up in the worst of what is to come. I will release her from the dark hour ahead. She will not be affected by what is coming.

MY bride is beautiful and prepared for ME, her KING and ROYAL BRIDEGROOM.

MY Eyes are only for her. Her beauty stuns ME. She ravishes ME with her radiance. She is a prepared people - ready to receive their BRIDEGROOM.

Song of Solomon 4:9. Thou hast ravished MY Heart, MY sister, MY spouse; thou hast ravished MY Heart with one of thine eyes, with one chain of thy neck.

They have prepared, made themselves ready. They are washed in MY Blood.

They are cleaned in MY Word. They are watching expectantly for ME. They are looking for ME daily. They are focused and fixed on ME. WE share intimacy with each other. WE know each other. MY people have laid their lives down before ME and have walked away from their desires for the world. They are sold out to ME only. They seek MY Face and MY Voice. They know MY Voice. I speak and they follow. They run after ME.

John 15:19. If ye were of the world, the world would love his own: but because ye are not of the world, but I have chosen you out of the world, therefore the world hateth you.

They are precious in MY Sight. I lead them and they follow. Their lives reflect MY Light to the world. They are the image of ME to the world, the lost, fading world.

Soon this beautiful light will be lifted out of the world and the only thing left will be darkness. The shadows will move in and take over. Darkness will consume the earth - all four corners. It will be a dark day indeed.

You needn't be here for that hour. You can follow after ME in full surrender. I will bring you to MYSELF, protect you, lead you out to safety, when I come for MY church, MY sweet church. She is ready and I will keep her from the dark hour ahead.

Children, it is almost time for MY approach. There is little time left. You must make ready. There is yet a little time remaining. Don't waste away this moment pursuing frivolous, worldly things. Give yourself time to make preparations.

Pursue ME with all your heart. Repent of all your sin. I want to hear true repentance of your sin-filled heart. The heart of a man deceives him. Only I can see the inner workings of a man's heart. I can see inside the chambers of a heart all the sin tucked away, hidden from sight.

Jeremiah 17:9. The heart is deceitful above all things, and desperately wicked: who can know it? Let ME clean your heart, wash it clean. Let ME purify your soul. Let ME make you ready to stand before ME. Only I can do this, MY children. Only I am capable.

Only I have the power to bring you to completion through MY Blood-Bought Ransom for your sins. This I long to give to you, make you white and wash you clean.

Acts 22:16. And now why tarriest thou? Arise and be baptized, and wash away thy sins, calling on the Name of the LORD.

Children, MY children, I wait upon you to come to ME in humble repentance, heart-felt repentance. Walk towards MY Light: receive MY Salvation, MY Blood- Bought Salvation. Let ME clean you, prepare you. Only I can do this for you. Lay down your life at MY Feet. Let ME have it in full. Don't be afraid. The world is collapsing. It holds no answers for you, no Truth. It is not reliable. Only I am the ROCK. Only I can be trusted with your life.

Give ME your life in full. Surrender it all to ME, not knowing what this may mean.

Give it up to ME and I will take it from you, care for you. I will make you MY OWN prize possession and fill you with MY Love, MY SPIRIT, and MY Peace. You will not fear the evil coming because MY Peace surpasses all your understanding. I bring Peace you can't comprehend. It is a supernatural Peace. It is being made right before GOD, a HOLY GOD. This is worth all of eternity to you. I can bring you to this...this insurmountable Peace.

Now is the hour to declare your faith for ME, to choose for ME. If you do not choose for ME, you choose for MY enemy. There are only two choices - only two. You are either for ME or against ME. There is no third position. Don't be deceived. If you ride the fence, you are not MINE. I want a full commitment.

Come before ME in complete, humble repentance and I will remove your sins as far as the east is from the west. I will never look upon them again. I will bring you to wholeness in ME. WE will share intimacy and you will know your GOD, truly know ME. I long for this "knowing" between US.

Psalms 103:12. As far as the east is from the west, so far hath HE removed our transgressions from us.

So come, come get to know ME. I am truly worth knowing. I will bring you to a place of peace and understanding. MY SPIRIT will guide you and open your eyes to Truth, life saving Truth. HE will show you the hour you are living in. You will be exposed to Truth like never before and then you can be saved and assured of a place in MY Kingdom.

This is what I long to bring to you.

Come get to know your GOD. Let US walk hand in hand. I will lead you out. Time is wasting. The hour is at hand. Choose for ME.

I am your LORD and SAVIOR GREAT MESSIAH HUMBLE KING YAHUSHUA.

CHAPTER 24

STOP FIGHTING WITH EACH OTHER

Let US begin. MY children, I have new Words for you.

All is not as it appears. Things are coming to a close the way you have known them. MY children, it is turning dark. All is turning dark. Life as you know it is changing dramatically. Soon, there will be no turning back, no chance for reprisal.

This is MY Warning. I am giving stern warnings and very few are heeding them, very few are paying attention, even listening.

Why are MY children not listening? They are caught up in their own worlds - not MY World, not MY Thoughts, not MY Warnings. This is serious, MY children. I am not putting out MY Warnings for MY good, but for your good. I know what is about to happen. I want you to know too.

Matthew 6:24. No man can serve two masters: for either he will hate the one, and love the other; or else he will hold to the one, and despise the other. Ye cannot serve GOD and mammon.

Children, I do not want you to remain in the dark. I want you to awaken to Truth. I want you to come alive to the reality of what is about to happen. Please awaken! Smell the evil - it is within your very senses. All has turned evil. No one embraces holiness. Everyone has turned astray.

Isaiah 53:6. All we like sheep have gone astray; we have turned everyone to his own way; and the LORD hath laid on HIM the iniquity of us all.

Only MY sweet bride remains faithful. Only she has eyes for ME. Only she looks fondly for ME, pursues ME at every turn. This is MY bride, MY church, MY true church.

Children, stop squabbling with each other. You are destroying each other. Stop arguing over MY Words. This is not the hour to be angry toward your fellow brothers and sisters. The enemy has come in and deceived you. He wants to bring you down to his level. Please stop the petty bickering among each other and love each other.

John 13:34. A new commandment I give unto you, That ye love one another; as I have loved you, that ye also love one another.

Repent for your sin toward each other. Bring blessings, not cursings to each other. This is not the hour to be fighting. Lay down your strife and come to ME.

I will show you how to get along with each other. MY children have fallen away because they fight with each other.

This is not the Way. This is not MY Way. Face ME children and repent. Then go to each other and make amends. Forgive one another. Time is wasting. Don't let these issues you have between you, bring you away from MY Eternal Salvation.

I want to rescue you MY children, but I can't save MY children who fight among each other. This cannot be. You are blocking your intimacy with ME when you withdraw your forgiveness for each other.

Matthew 6:14. But if ye forgive men their trespasses, your Heavenly FATHER will also forgive you: So forgive and forgive completely, keeping no record of each other's harms and trespasses. This is MY Way children, the Way of a HOLY GOD. Put your grievances aside that you hold for each other and come to ME in repentance.

Matthew 6:15. But if ye forgive not men their trespasses, neither will your FATHER forgive your trespasses.

I want to free you of this sin. There is no sin on this earth that is worth losing your eternal salvation over. Please remember this. Children, MY Love is great, but I cannot overlook sin. So repent today and forgive each other. Run to do this. Leave nothing undone. Forgive all, so that I, your FATHER in Heaven can forgive you. This is so simple, yet so few grasp the importance of forgiveness and releasing past hurts.

Let ME care for your past pain. Put your sorrows on MY Shoulders and let ME bring you to healing. Only I can do this. Come to ME and let ME bear these burdens. I will do it. I am willing.

Let ME rebuild your life and repair your pain. Bring your pain to ME. Forgive those who have hurt you and turn to ME for relief from your pain. I am willing to bring you to completion and wholeness of heart. These are MY Promises.

Read MY Word. I am a GOD of restoration. Let ME Restore you to wholeness and gladness. I am the ONE WHO Restores and makes Whole—no other. Let ME show you True Love. Only I offer True Love.

Joel 2:25. And I will restore to you the years that the locust hath eaten, the cankerworm, and the caterpillar, and the palmerworm, MY great army which I sent among you.

Yes, this hour is closing in for MY Return. Let ME clean you up and restore you to new life in ME. Let ME prepare you for MY Coming. I am ready and willing. I am your HOPE, only HOPE.

Come to ME. Now is the time. Don't wait too long. Only I am worthy. Worthy is the LAMB. Run into MY Arms, quickly.

This is your LORD, YAHUSHUA.

CHAPTER 25

I WILL NOT TAKE YOU
IF YOU HAVE UNREPENTANT SIN

Let US begin. I am ready to give you more Words: Children, the hour is nearing for MY Soon Return. It comes right on schedule.

Many think I am not coming ever. Many think I will not come for many years. MY children, I am coming very soon. MY Approach is near. Even at the door. It will catch many off guard. Many will be asleep when I come, spiritually asleep.

1 Thessalonians 5:6. Therefore let us not sleep; as do others; but let us watch and be sober.

Soon, this time is coming. Only those who are watching and waiting will be ready.

All those who are not paying attention will be left to face what is coming. The time is very close.

Children, you need to be ready. Don't be caught unawares. I do not want to leave anyone behind, but sadly many will be left. What a sad hour is coming. I want you to awaken. Come to terms with this reality. I am approaching and I am even at the door. Soon, no one will be surprised anymore as reality will set in as to what has happened. The world will know that change has come to it, great changes. It will not be the same place very soon.

MY children, listen to ME closely, I will not take you if you have unrepentant sin.

I cannot take you with ME. It cannot be, MY children. So come before ME and repent of your sin. Please make this a priority.

Luke 13:5. I tell you, Nay: but except ye repent, ye shall all likewise perish.

Come make things right with ME. I desire to bring you into MY Kingdom. I want to rescue you from what is coming. I cannot take you, if you are not MINE. If you have not come before ME, and given your life to ME, you are not MINE. This is very important children. You need to give your life over to ME. Lay it down at MY Feet, holding nothing back.

This is the time to come before ME in humble repentance. Bring your cares and worries to ME... I want your life. I will exchange your life with all its imperfections and troubles, for a life of love, joy, and completion.

Soon, very soon, I am coming and you want to be ready. This hour is closing in.

Let ME bring you to MY Completion and restore you to wholeness. MY Love can cover all of your sins. Come to ME, I am waiting with open Arms, Arms that long to hold you and to love you.

Luke 5:31. And JESUS answering said unto them, They that are whole need not a physician; but they that are sick.

Don't delay. This is an important hour. I will not be late to remove MY bride.

I am ready to take her home to the mansions I have prepared for her. This is where she will go for safekeeping.

So MY children, make yourselves ready, as MY Coming is nearly nigh. I am speaking to you as a FATHER WHO Loves and Cares for you. I want to save you, to rescue you from a world soon to go mad. Let ME show you the door to safety. It is opening soon. But then it will close. So be ready, as I am ready to receive you.

This is your LORD GOD from Heaven, YAHUSHUA.

CHAPTER 26

STAY FOCUSED ON ME

Luke 13:24-25. Strive to enter in at the strait gate: for many, I say unto you, will seek to enter in, and shall not be able. When once the master of the house is risen up, and hath shut to the door, and ye begin to stand without, and to knock at the door, saying, LORD, LORD, open unto us; and he shall answer and say unto, I know you not whence ye are: Let US begin again: Children, this is your LORD Speaking.

I want you to stay focused on ME, eyes fixed on ME. Now is not the time to be running to and fro and focused on the world. This is the hour of discernment and focus. This is the hour to be paying attention and watching for ME and MY Soon Return. Each day it draws nearer.

Do not discount MY Warnings. These Warnings are coming from all sides. I am sending messages from many directions. They are coming through disasters, through wars and rumors of wars, through MY prophets and messengers, through signs and wonders in the skies, through the mouths of babes. You will be without excuse if you are left behind. You will have no one to blame but yourself if you are left to face the worst.

MY Book has been clear about the times you are living in and what is about to take place on this earth. Children, you must awaken to these Truths. Don't stand empty-handed believing I gave you nothing to go by and no warnings. I gave you MY Book, but if you refuse and ignore MY Words and Warnings, I can't help you.

I have been clear and prolific in MY Messages given out. You will stand before ME without excuse if you refuse to receive these messages. I can plead, cajole, request for you to pay attention, but I will never force you in making this decision.

The choice is strictly yours.

2 Peter 3:3-4. Knowing this first, that there shall come in the last days scoffers, walking after their own lusts, And saying, Where is the promise of HIS coming? For since the fathers fell asleep, all things continue as they were from the beginning of creation.

So few will make the right choice or even choose at all. No choice is still a choice for MY enemy. Sadly many will not choose and still remain under his power and control. This saddens ME deeply as I paid a large price on the Hill of Calvary so that MY children can experience freedom, true freedom from the clutches of MY enemy and theirs. It is not necessary for MY children to suffer needlessly in this life or the next without hope and love everlasting.

Matthew 24:37-39. But as the days of Noah were, so shall also the coming of the SON of man be. For as in the days that were before the flood they were eating and drinking, marrying and giving in marriage, until the day that Noah entered into the ark, And knew not until the flood came, and took them all away; so shall also the coming of the SON of man be.

So children, awaken! Take this, O' so Precious Gift, I offer and let ME purchase your freedom. I can do it. I am willing. It is MINE to give and I give it freely to you. It is MY Pleasure to bring you into wholeness, peace, and a sound mind. All these are yours if you turn to ME, make a full surrender, lay your life down at MY Feet. Let ME be your LORD and MASTER. Let ME fill you with MY SPIRIT and cover you with MY Blood so that I can wipe out your sin record.

Luke 17:16. And fell down on his face at HIS Feet, giving HIM thanks: and he was a Samaritan.

Let ME show you the Way to walk in and release you from the ways of the enemy.

Come to ME and receive a heart that is purified and refined in MY Fire and washed in the water of MY Word. This is yours for the taking.

John 15:3. Now ye are clean through the Word which I have spoken unto you.

Walk away from all your plans and give ME your life, even all your plans. Let ME have your life. I will replace your life and plans with MY Perfect Plans and Will for your life - the plans that were meant for your life that I purposed for you, when I created you. Walk in MY Will, sin no more by walking in your own will. Come into MY Will and be perfect before ME. This is MY Desire for your life.

I am your CREATOR. I know what is best for you. Come and receive this Great Gift - Peace with your CREATOR.

Children, the hour is hastening. Do not waste a lot of time in moving on this decision. Time is of the essence. I do not want you to face the worst. Seek ME and I will show you this Truth and open your eyes. I will pull the scales off and make you free, prepare you to come home with ME to safety.

Acts 9:17-18. And Ananias went his way, and entered into the house; and putting his hands on him said, Brother Saul, the LORD, even JESUS, that appeared unto thee in the way as thou camest, hath sent me, that thou mightiest receive thy sight, and be filled with the HOLY GHOST. And immediately there fell from his eyes as it had been scales: and he received sight forthwith, and arose, and was baptized.

I want you to awaken. This is MY Desire, for you to come into MY Waiting Arms.

Don't hesitate. Hesitation can be dangerous and may cost you your eternal salvation.

These Words come from Your FATHER WHO Cares, Loving YAHUSHUA.

CHAPTER 27

YOU MUST BE MADE READY,
IF YOU WANT TO COME OUT WITH ME

Let US begin. Children I am your LORD and I have Words for you.

Time is winding down. Soon I will be coming to get MY bride to bring her out to safety, safekeeping. She will rise out of the earth in triumph and glory. She is MY overcomer. I will bring her to MYSELF, raise her up to meet ME in the air.

This Event is called "The Rapture," but whatever you choose to call it - this Event is happening soon. I will pull MY bride free from the chains of a world about to go awry - completely out of control, a world living apart from GOD.

1 Corinthians 15:51-52. 51Behold, I shew you a mystery; We shall not all sleep, but we shall be changed, 52In a moment, in the twinkling of an eye, at the last trump: for the trumpet shall sound, and the dead shall be raised incorruptible, and we shall be changed.

I am a GOD of control and now the world will experience life without MY Great Hand of Protection over it. Soon, this will take place.

Many will witness this Event as those left behind. Fewer will witness it as those who are taken out of the earth. I want you to be one of those who are rescued, but you must be made ready if you want to come out with ME. Only those who have washed themselves white in MY Blood and who are avidly watching for MY Soon Return will be coming with ME, when I call MY bride up hither. Only a few will be coming. This is serious, MY children, all others will stay behind.

1 John 1:7. But if we walk in the light, as HE is in the light, we have fellowship with one another, and the Blood of JESUS CHRIST HIS SON cleanseth us from all sin.

What sadness awaits them, those who are left. Don't be one of them. You do not have to be. I have made a Way for you. I have cleared a passage. It is with MY Blood that I have made a way. Your way is clear and free through ME. There is no other way.

No one else will save you. There are no other answers. Only this: turn to ME, surrender to ME. Don't hesitate. Do this quickly, as MY Coming is near. Make time to get to know ME. I am ready and waiting for you. MY Love waits on you.

Come to ME in humble repentance. I will make you ready through MY Blood Covering and MY Word - the washing of MY Word.

Ephesians 5:25-27. 25Husbands, love your wives, even as CHRIST also loved the church, and gave HIMSELF for it; 26That HE might sanctify and cleanse it with the washing of water by the Word, 27That HE might present it to HIMSELF a glorious church, not having spot, or wrinkle, or any such thing; but that it should be holy and without blemish.

Come to ME. Don't waste any time. This is the hour to get serious with GOD.

Don't wait too long.

I am your LORD GOD YAHUSHUA.

CHAPTER 28

YOUR ETERNITY IS IN THE BALANCE

Let US begin again. The time is at hand children, for MY Near Return. It is closing in.

There is much to do to be prepared. I have much for you to do. I need you to submit your life over to ME in complete submission, total surrender. I want it all, children. A half-way commitment is no commitment. Please consider this seriously. Your eternity is in the balance. Without this full surrender, you are not truly MINE, no matter what you say or think; only by a full surrender are you truly MINE.

Children, I want you to stay focused on ME, all eyes on ME. I know the way out. I know the directions to the escape route: Only ME. I am the ONE WHO holds the key to your rescue, your retrieval from what is to come.

If you look to the left or the right, you will be distracted. Don't let it happen. The hour is waning. MY children you must awaken. Come to your senses. Stay alert!

Matthew 7:14. Because strait is the gate, and narrow is the way, which leadeth unto life, and few there be that find it.

The time is coming for ME to retrieve MY bride, to bring her home with ME, to escort her to her new homes, where she will reside for eternity with ME, her BRIDEGROOM.

I long to take her into MY Arms, hold her close and pour MY Love over her, to adore her, and show her MY Love. Soon this will take place. I am ready and MY bride has made herself ready. She waits patiently.

MY bride is the light of this world. She shines bright in a dark, ugly world. She is the last remaining light. Her light is intense and reflects MY Light. This Light is Truth - MY Truth everlasting. Everything else is lies from the enemy. He has deluded the world with his lies and half-truths. The world is deceived and the people cannot see the Truth.

Jeremiah 17:5-6. 5Thus saith the LORD; Cursed be the man that trusteth in man, and maketh flesh his arm, and whose heart departeth from the LORD. 6For he shall be like the heath in the desert, and shall not see when good cometh; but shall inhabit the parched places in the wilderness, in a salt land and not inhabited.

The time has come for MY children to wake up, face the Truth. The world is coming to a close as it has been. A new age is dawning: the age of the antichrist and the hostile changes that will follow. No one will be safe, only MY true followers who I take home with ME, when I pull them out to safety. These are the only ones who are exempt from what is coming - what the world will face once MY enemy comes into power and is allowed to rule and reign. What a dark day lies ahead.

Revelation 17:16-17. And the ten horns which thou sawest upon the beast, these shall hate the whore, and shall make her desolate and naked, and shall eat her flesh, and burn her with fire. For GOD hath put in their hearts to fulfill HIS Will, and to agree, and give their kingdom unto the beast, until the Words of GOD shall be fulfilled.

This will be a gravely dark time for mankind, deep darkness and trouble is coming.

This hour that is coming is coming at a rapid rate. Soon nothing will be the same.

I want you children to be ready to ascend out of the earth with ME. I want you to come with ME. You can avoid all that is coming to the earth if you remove your blinders and come to ME in humble repentance and certain surrender.

I long to take you into MY Arms and save you from all the grief that lies ahead, it is MY Greatest Desire to save you from the coming hour of trouble.

I am giving out many Words and signs to bring you to this Truth. Few are paying attention. Too many are still married to this harlot world and all its evil. Yes, children as long as you cling to the world and its ways you are committing adultery against ME and I cannot have you in MY Kingdom. So come away MY children. Walk away from the world and all she stands for. She is vile and immoral, anti-GOD, and I cannot tolerate this world anymore.

Ezekiel 16:35-36. Wherefore, O' harlot, hear the Word of the LORD: Thus saith the LORD GOD; Because thy filthiness was poured out, and they nakedness discovered through thy whoredoms with thy lovers, and with all the idols of thy abominations, and by the blood of thy children, which thou didst give unto them; Time is wasting. Come to your senses. Open your eyes. See the times you are living in. Don't be fooled by what looks normal and right.

I will bring you into MY Kingdom for eternity. Make a full surrender to ME. Make ME your LORD and MASTER. The time is now for this decision. No delays! This is your LORD and MASTER, YAHUSHUA.

Luke 21:31-32. So likewise ye, when ye see these things come to pass, know ye that the Kingdom of GOD is nigh at hand. Verily I say unto you, This generation shall not pass away, till all be fulfilled.

CHAPTER 29

YOUR MUST RUN, NOT WALK TO ME NOW

Yes daughter, Let US begin. MY children, this is your LORD Speaking.

I want you to know that I am coming very soon. The hour is right at the door.

Soon I will make MY Way to come and get MY bride. She is lovely and her beauty is radiant.

I look on her with great desire and I am anxious to bring her home with ME to her beautiful heavenlies and the home I have prepared for her. This hour approaches, MY children. You need to make ready. You need to hasten to preparations.

There is a dark day looming. Soon I will carry off MY bride. I will pull her aside to safety. This is moments away. MY Return is nearly at the door. So come into MY Waiting Arms MY children, very soon.

You must run, not walk to ME now. Don't be complacent children. Don't treat this with disdain as MY Warnings are real. I am bringing you to this place, MY children; I want you to awaken, to come to life, to face the Truth. Very soon this hour is even at the door.

Listen to ME children, I want you to awaken. There is trouble coming to the earth. It is coming like a locomotive. It is barreling down. Nothing can stop it.

No man, no woman, no child can stop what is coming.

There will be stern consequences for those who disregard MY Warnings. I have put out many warnings in many ways, O' so many warnings. You will be without excuse if you say you never knew.

Everyone is accountable for their own sin - as I have been clear in MY Book. It is all spelled out in MY Book if MY children would bother to read it. It takes time to read MY Book. Something you do *for the world and pursuit of the world must be put aside to find time for MY Book. But you will not put aside your worldly pursuits to make time for MY Word.

Romans 14:12. So then every one of us shall give account of himself to GOD.

You would rather play with the world. But all that glitters is not gold, MY children.

The world looks all shiny and new, but it is pure poison and it only offers death.

Put the world aside and face your GOD. Am I not worth pursuing?

John 12:25. He that loveth his life shall lose it; and he that hateth his life in this world shall keep it unto life eternal.

Yes, I died for you a grievous death on a horrible wooden cross. It was excruciating. Yes, I released MY Life over to MY FATHER after hours of torment at the hands of evil, immoral, hateful men who were doing the will of their father, MY enemy. This was the price I paid for you and your life. Am I not worth your time, your love, and attention?

Psalms 22:12-18. Many bulls have compassed ME: strong bulls of Bashan have beset ME round. They gaped upon ME with their mouths, as a ravening and a roaring lion. I am poured out like water, and all MY Bones are out of joint: MY Heart is like wax; it is melted in the midst of MY Bowels. MY Strength is dried up like a potsherd; and MY Tongue cleaveth to MY Jaws; and thou hast brought ME into the dust of death. For dogs have compassed ME: the assembly of the wicked have enclosed ME: they pierced MY Hands and MY Feet. I may tell all MY Bones: they look and stare upon ME. They part MY Garments among them, and cast lots upon MY Vesture.

Come to ME. I ask you to come to ME. Let ME take you in MY Arms to hold you, caress you as MY own. I am your FATHER WHO Loves you. No greater love is there than MINE - no higher affection than

MINE for you. Do not deny ME your love. Come to ME in humble repentance. Let ME Clean you up, make you right before ME. Let ME fill your heart with joy and gladness. I can do it. I am willing.

Now is the time. Do not wait or hesitate. This is the day of MY Return. I am coming to bring you out. Let ME fill you with MY SPIRIT. Let me make you whole: make you complete in ME. Time is wasting, children. Soon there will be no time left. So don't discount this wondrous offer of MY Sweet Salvation and the Blood I shed for your redemption so that you might be whole and complete in ME perpetually, for all eternity.

Matthew 25:46. And these shall go away into everlasting punishment: but the righteous into life eternal.

I long to know you intimately, WE can have this closeness. It is yours for the taking. Ask ME and I will give it to you. I long to share intimacy with you, to have a closeness, it is MY Desire to be near you always in a deep and personal way.

If you come to ME in this way I will come to you also. MY Word sets out that I require this intimacy of you. I want you to seek ME in a quiet place where WE can share each other's company.

MY children, this is where I can give you instructions on how I want you to live out your life. When you come to ME in intimacy then WE can begin to know each other and I can lay out MY Plans before you of how I want you to lead your life.

But first, you must be in MY Will and to be in MY Will you must surrender your life to ME - give ME your all in all. Turn your life over to ME and hold nothing back - make your life fully MINE. I want it in complete surrender. This means forsaking all others and the world. I want you to walk away from your commitment to the world and be willing to follow ME wherever I lead you.

This is not something most people want to do. So many want to cling to something that they refuse to let go of. MY children, what are you putting between US? Is it your work, your wealth? Is it your ministry? Is it your children? What are you putting between US? What excites you more than ME?

Matthew 10:37-39. 37He that loveth father or mother more than ME is not worthy of ME: and he that loveth son or daughter more than ME is not worthy of ME. 38And he that taketh not his cross, and followeth after ME, is not worthy of ME. 39He that findeth his life shall lose it: and he that loseth his life for MY sake shall find it.

Children, if you do not put ME first, you will lose whatever excites you more than ME and ME also. These are serious Words MY children, but necessary to say. I want you to hear them and consider where you are in ME. Am I first place or am I a lower rung in your life? MY children, you need to evaluate your position in ME. What place do I hold in your heart? Children, stand near ME - I long to hold you close to MY Heart. The hour is coming for MY Soon Return. I don't want you to be left behind to face the worst. Come and find ME. I am always near, waiting on you to pursue ME. MY Love is Great! Don't miss the enjoyment of MY Love for eternity.

This is your ROYAL BRIDEGROOM, YAHUSHUA.

CHAPTER 30

MY BRIDE IS LOVELY IN ALL HER WAYS

Yes daughter, Let US begin again. MY children it is I, your LORD. I greet you in the Name of the MY FATHER, your FATHER.

Children, the hour is hastening for the descent for MY Retrieval of the bride. She is lovely in all her ways. I am pleased to call her MY own. She is MY beloved.

I will take her into MY Awaiting Arms very soon. She will be with ME for all eternity.

WE will be like shooting stars, she and I. OUR Love will never know an end, endless, eternal love. The peace I bring her will last forever. She is MY sweet bride. She is obedient and loves MY Ways. She is MY love and follows ME. She walks in MY Narrow Path. She watches for ME. Her ways are lovely.

She is the last remaining light to the world. She shows the world MY Ways. The world sees ME in her. She reflects MY Image to the world. Her ways are humble and reflecting childlike faith. These are the qualities of those in heaven.

The hour approaches for ME to withdraw her from the earth. I am taking her to MYSELF. I am putting her away in safety. Soon, she will come with ME to safety where I will keep her away from things to come. This hour approaches, do not doubt.

Matthew 18:3. And said, Verily I say unto you, Except ye be converted, and become as little children, ye shall not enter into the Kingdom of Heaven.

I want you to prepare and make ready as MY bride is ready. She has made herself ready, washing herself in MY Blood. She has cleaned herself and is spot and wrinkle-free. She is ready to come to MY Heavenlies, to commune with ME and enjoy MY Presence.

Ephesians 5:25-27. 25Husbands, love your wives, even as CHRIST also loved the church, and gave HIMSELF for it; 26That HE might sanctify and cleanse it with the washing of water by the Word, 27That HE might present it to HIMSELF a glorious church, not having spot, or wrinkle, or any such thing; but that it should be holy and without blemish.

I am ready for her to come to ME in the skies, to come up hither. This is a mystery, a great mystery, as she will be changed to perfection. She will be made like MY Image in a glorious new body.

Her body will be changed: no flaws, imperishable, eternal light, MY Light. She will shine in the Heavenlies. She will be glorious and radiant as WE share the same qualities. This body will never die or ever know death. It is an eternal fountain of youth. This body will know no limitations. MY children will enjoy their new bodies. They will never experience pain. These bodies will change with the circumstance required by it. They will navigate throughout heaven effortlessly.

These bodies will fly or walk. They will do everything the human body does and so much more. They are bodies of light. These bodies will never be hindered the way human bodies are. There is nothing these bodies can't do. There are no limitations like that of a human body. MY children will eat and enjoy food just as they do now. Everything about these new glorified bodies will startle and amaze those receiving them. All will change in a breath, in a moment.

MY children will change in a moment. It will happen quickly for them. They will be astounded. Children this is an eternal change. Eye has not seen or ear has not heard what I have prepared for MY children, MY faithful children.

1 Corinthians 15:51-54. 51Behold, I shew you a mystery; We shall not all sleep, but we shall all be changed, 52In a moment, in the twinkling of an eye, at the last trump: for the trumpet shall sound, and the dead shall be raised incorruptible, and we shall be changed.

53For this corruptible must put on incorruption, and this mortal must put on immortality. 54So when this corruptible shall have put on incorruption, and this mortal shall have put on immortality, then shall be brought to pass the saying that is written, Death is swallowed up in victory.

Turn and face ME. You do not want to miss this event and all MY Glory, when I come to receive MY bride unto MYSELF. This event is coming. Children prepare - make preparations. Be vigilant, pursue ME. Very few are watching for ME. They are caught in the clutches of the world.

It all looks so normal and right, but she is deceptive. The world is a liar. She is full of evil and embraces her own truth. She clings to the lies she deals in and passes it off as truth. There is no Truth in her mouth. The world would have you believe all is well but all is not well. Soon, the world will understand this very well.

Make yourselves ready. I will not wait long now. MY Coming is right at the door.

I stand at the door and knock. Let ME into your heart. The hour is shifting. The sand in the glass is waning.

Get out of your comfort zone and get on your knees. Repent of your sin. Turn your life over to ME and I will clean you, make you ready, I long to do this. Set yourselves apart from the world. Come apart, come away. She is death. She will not continue on apart from ME. Her downfall is turning her back to ME and seeking her own evil way.

1 Thessalonians 5:23. And the very GOD of peace sanctify you wholly; and I pray GOD your whole spirit and soul and body be preserved blameless unto the coming of our LORD JESUS CHRIST.

No children, you must choose. Do you go with her or come out with ME? This is your choice to make. I cannot make it for you. I can only request that you come with ME.

I want you to be by MY Side for eternity. I long for you to join ME in MY Heavenlies. But this is your choice to make. Surrender to ME or stay behind. I await your decision. MY Love is patient, but soon I must rescue MY bride. These Words are sure. I am a GOD WHO does not lie. Come to ME before it is too late.

The Great "I AM" YAHUSHUA.

CHAPTER 31

VERY FEW WORSHIP ME AND REPENT TO ME

So Let US begin again (February 28, 2012). MY children who I cherish, the hour approaches for MY Return. You will need to make preparations. You will need to be ready. Ready yourself. I want you to cover yourself in MY Blood.

The world is closing down. It is reaching its demise. It is coming to a close of its former self. It is escalating into moral decay. It is rising up into pure evil. It is turning its back solidly against its GOD. Very few seek ME on the level I desire by MY children. Very few throw themselves at MY Feet and worship ME and repent to ME. Very few are willing to follow ME wherever I want them to go without reservation.

Mark 8:34. And when HE had called the people unto HIM with his disciples also, HE said unto them, Whosoever will come after ME, let him deny himself, and take up his cross, and follow ME.

Too many are caught up in the world and their worldly pursuits. Don't you know this world is an enmity to ME? I am not going to tolerate this world much longer.

I will not allow it to carry on. Soon I will remove MY bride and pull MY children away to safety. She is beautiful and I am ready for her to come to the home I have prepared for her in the Heavenlies. This is surely going to happen soon, MY children. You need to be aware. You need to awaken to this Truth.

So many are dozing, sound asleep. They are drifting away from ME. They are falling into enemy hands and soon like birds caught off guard they will fall into the fowler's net.

Psalm 124:7. Our soul is escaped as a bird out of the snare of the fowlers: the snare is broken, and we are escaped.

Awaken to these Truths, MY children. Wake and behold, I am coming! Awaken before you are caught completely off guard and fall away completely. The hour approaches for MY Return and so many are still sleeping - sound asleep. This is not the hour to be caught unawares. You must wake! Soon the enemy will have you right where he wants you if you don't come to ME in a full surrender. This is the time to be serious with your GOD.

I am a Patient GOD, but MY Patience will soon run out. I will no longer tolerate this dying world, dying because it resoundly rejects its GOD. Every corner of the world has rejected ME. It is unilateral rejection. The world now embraces evil.

It hugs evil, it sleeps with evil. It rises to do evil; it lies down to do evil. Only MY bride truly follows ME. Only she is faithful. Only she has kept her hands clean.

Only she pursues ME and has come apart from the world. Only she has not sullied her clothes by partaking in the things of the world.

She is MY Light in a dark world. She shines bright in the darkness. Her light casts a gleam out into a dark world, a world growing ever darker daily.

Soon this light will be extinguished as I must remove her to safety. Then the world will grow ever darker and bleak. This is a dark hour, MY children.

You must step into MY Light while you still have a chance. There is little time remaining. The hour is almost up. The minute hand is about to strike midnight.

Don't take these Words casually. They are for your benefit: to save you from the worst; to save you from what is coming.

John 8:12. Then spake JESUS again unto them, saying, I am the LIGHT of the world: he that followeth ME shall not walk in darkness, but shall have the LIGHT of Life.

MY children, I love you as only a loving father would. I want you to come into MY Arms where you will be safe. It is only through ME that you will find safety only in and through ME will you be saved. There is no other way. If you turn to the world for answers you will be misled by turning only by the leadings of men, men who know nothing of ME or MY Truth.

This hour is nearing MY children. Come apart from the world. Wash your hands of the filth she brings you to. She is leading you away from ME. Come in close to ME. Keep your eyes fixed on ME. I am the Last Rescue coming before the world totally comes apart. Don't miss this ONE Sure Rescue to safety.

James 4:8. Draw nigh to GOD, and HE will draw nigh to you. Cleanse your hands, ye sinners; and purify your hearts, ye double minded.

Get ready to be among MY bride. Come to ME in full surrender. Lay your life down at MY Feet. Give ME your allegiance, your all. I will guide you out safely.

This is MY Promise to you - safe passage, freedom from what's soon coming to the earth.

Don't turn MY Offer down. Don't live to regret your decisions. I am true to MY Word. I can deliver you to safety. I am a Strong GOD, faithful to deliver. Let not your heart be troubled. Run into MY Saving Arms.

Your Faithful GOD, YAHUSHUA.

CHAPTER 32

I AM ABOUT TO REMOVE MY BRIDE TO SAFETY

MY daughter, Let US begin (February 28, 2012). Children, I am your GOD. I am a GOD WHO cares deeply for you. I only want the best for you.

Now MY children, I want you to hear MY Words. Listen closely, the world is about to turn upside down. Soon the world will be turning inside out. There will be much that will happen in and around the world and very little of it will be good. I am lifting MY Protective Hand from the world, because she has revolted against ME. She walks in the opposite direction of MY Heart, MY Ways, MY Truth.

She is an abomination to ME. I am about to allow the dogs of satan to take over the world.

Psalm 22:16. For dogs have compassed ME: the assembly of the wicked have enclosed ME: they pierced MY Hands and MY Feet.

This event has nearly arrived. MY children, these are dark days coming. I will not tolerate much more evil from this world. I am about to remove MY bride to safety. She is coming out very soon. I will not put up with this world much longer. I am about to spue this world out. The evil that has taken over this world is putrid in MY Face. I can no longer look upon it. I will not allow MY dear ones to tolerate much of it any longer either.

MY church is about to be removed out to safety. This hour is coming quickly.

Why do you children doubt so? Where is your faith? Why are you so doubtful? Whether you believe or not has no bearing on what is about to happen. It will happen, MY children just as MY Book sets out that it will. I have been truthful in all MY Words. I have described the end times in MY Book. Read MY Words, familiarize yourself with MY Book. Read these Words carefully. You will see that these are, in fact, the end times and MY Coming is near.

Children stop listening to each other and come seek ME. Come to ME with sincereness of heart and I will show you the Truth, I long to reveal Truth to you.

I do not mislead MY children. But if they choose not to seek ME then I cannot reveal Truth to them. They will continue to go down blind alleyways and paths of destruction.

Come with ME and find your way. I will lead you to MY, O' so narrow, path. Few find it, MY children few look for it. Don't be among the many who never find this path. There are so many lost on the wayside, so many on the broad road paved with destruction.

Matthew 7:13. Enter ye in at the strait gate: for wide is the gate, and broad is the way, that leadeth to destruction, and many there be which go in thereat: Come to your senses, MY children, come alive. Seek ME hard. This is the hour to come to life, to come to life in ME. There are no other routes to freedom and life everlasting.

Now is the hour, now! Run into MY Waiting Arms. Don't hesitate. Hesitation will be your ending and sure demise. I want to save you. Surrender your all to ME. Give ME every bit of you. I want it all. Partial surrender is not sufficient.

Come to ME and lay your life down. I will receive it and glorify you for MY Own purposes to serve ME and enjoy Heaven for eternity.

Jeremiah 30:19. And out of them shall proceed thanksgiving and the voice of them that make merry: and I will multiply them, and they shall not be few; I will also glorify them, and they shall not be small.

This hour is running out. MY enemy is making his way to the scene. Soon there will be no denying the hour you live in, but then it may be too late for your rescue and you will have missed your opportunity to be saved. MY children, I am trying to wake you up and bring you to the Truth. What must I do to get your attention? If you wait too long to come to ME, you will be left behind. I will be forced to leave you. Don't let this happen.

Repentance, surrender, and intimacy: this is what I desire; this is what I require of you. These are the requirements to be admitted into MY Kingdom. Does MY Book not say this? Come now before it is too late. Come and I will clean you in MY Blood and you will be ready to stand before ME and be received into MY Kingdom, MY Everlasting Kingdom of beauty.

Revelation 1:5. And from JESUS CHRIST, WHO is the FAITHFUL WITNESS, and the FIRST BEGOTTEN of the dead, and the PRINCE of the kings of the earth. Unto HIM that loved us, and washed us from our sins in HIS OWN blood, Time is wasting. Do not waste another minute on this world.

This is your LORD and KING Speaking, HIGH and MIGHTY ETERNAL AUTHORITY LORD YAHUSHUA.

CHAPTER 33

I WANT FIRST PLACE OR NO PLACE

Let US begin (March 1, 2012). Children this is your LORD. I have new Words to bring to your attention: MY children, there is a new age about to dawn over this earth. It is one marked by evil: evil men, evil times. You must prepare to make your departure with ME. I want you to make ready. I will need to pull MY bride out of this evil world and put her away to safety.

I cannot keep her in this world much longer, because soon this world will become very ugly and foreboding. She must be put aside to safety. Then the world will unleash its evil to those who remain behind.

Soon, this event will take place. Even now, all the storm fronts are coming together to create a perfect storm of destruction, a wave of terror that will soon overwhelm all of mankind who choose against ME.

I must be made first in your life. I must have first place so that you can avoid this horror. I am not a GOD WHO wishes to see MY children suffer, but if you refuse to put ME above the idols you place in your hearts above ME, then you will soon learn what it means to reject your GOD, your CREATOR.

I am not a GOD WHO can be toyed with. I want first place or no place. I do not care to be second place or third place on your list of priorities. I created you for MY Benefit to Worship, to Glorify, and to Know ME, I long to relate with you in an intimate way to have close relationship with ME.

If you choose not to know ME in this way, then you can have your way, then WE can part company and you can have company with MY enemy in his eternal destination. I am a Jealous GOD. I did not create you to share you with MY enemy.

Deuteronomy 32:16. They provoked HIM to jealousy with strange gods, with abominations provoked they HIM to anger.

You either want to be MINE exclusively or you can follow the broad path to destruction where so many others have already gone. Very few want to get to know ME above all their worldly pursuits.

Where do I stand in your life? Am I not worthy of a first place position in your heart? I died for you MY children, a horrible, painful death. I created you and give you life. I sustain you every day. MY children, soon you will need to decide.

Do you want MY Peace, Calm, and Love? Do you want MY Assurance of safe passage out of a world soon to come apart? Then now is the hour to decide what you will choose to do. How will you embrace your GOD... with love and devotion or with tepid indifference?

Philippians 2:8. And being found in fashion as a man, HE humbled HIMSELF, and became obedient unto death, even the death of the cross.

I need you to decide. Are you willing to die to yourself for ME and surrender your all to ME? I am waiting for you to respond to MY Offer to come to ME in humble repentance to ask ME to forgive your sins and to cover you in MY Blood. It is only by MY Blood that you can be saved, only by the sacrifices I made on the cross.

If you accept this Gift of MY Blood Ransom, repent of your sins with sincerity of heart. Lay your life down before ME. Follow ME without hesitation. I can turn your life around, clean you up and prepare you for MY Kingdom. Make you ready to come with ME.

Consider this offer seriously. Children you can only wait so long. Waiting to see what will happen and avoiding this decision could cause you to lose all that I have for you in the next life. Don't be foolish, come to your senses. Make ready, be ready. I want you to be saved from the horrors ahead.

I am praying for you. I am praying to MY FATHER on your behalf. Children this hour is dwindling. I want you to decide. I WILL COME FOR MY BRIDE! Don't miss this great move of GOD. Don't miss everything I have for you.

I am true to MY Word. I WILL PREVAIL AND MY CHURCH WILL PREVAIL! So you MUST heed MY Words.

I am the Great "I AM" I am the LORD YAHUSHUA FAITHFUL TO DELIVER.

CHAPTER 34

THERE IS TRIBULATION COMING - GREAT TRIBULATION

Let US begin (March 2, 2012). MY children, it is I, your LORD. I have new Words to give you: Children, this is a serious hour. There is much grief coming to the world. There will be much peril and sadness. These troubles have already begun. Sin is rampant among the people.

Do not despair though, I have overcome the world. I am coming to remove MY bride to safety. She is beautiful and lovely to behold. She watches for MY Return, MY Soon Return. She keeps her eyes fixed on ME. I love her with all MY Heart. I embrace her with MY Eyes. I watch her every move. She never leaves MY Sight.

Soon she will be with ME in MY Heavenlies tucked away safely while the world she leaves comes apart at the seams.

John 16:33. These things I have spoken unto you, that in ME ye might have peace. In the world ye shall have tribulation: but be of good cheer; I have overcome the world.

This event is unfolding now children. There is tribulation coming - great tribulation. Nothing like the world has ever witnessed before. You all seem to be so complacent about MY Warnings, MY Signs, MY Book.

Do you not understand that trouble is coming to the earth? It is coming and no man can stop it. This stems from a world that is abandoning its GOD, rejecting its GOD. This world has no regard for ME and MY Ways. So I must pull away MY Protective Hand and retreat with MY bride. Soon the world will understand what real terror means.

1 John 4:1-8. 1Beloved, believe not every spirit, but try the spirits whether they are of GOD: because many false prophets are gone out into the world. 2Hereby know ye the SPIRIT of GOD: Every spirit that confesseth that JESUS CHRIST is come in the flesh is of GOD:

3And every spirit that confesseth not that JESUS CHRIST is come in the flesh is not of GOD: and this is that spirit of antichrist, whereof ye have heard that it should come; and even now already is it in the world. 4Ye are of GOD, little children, and have overcome them: because greater is HE that is in you, than he that is in the world. 5They are of the world: therefore speak they of the world, and the world heareth them. 6We are of GOD: he that knoweth GOD heareth us; he that is not of GOD heareth not us. Hereby know the SPIRIT of Truth, and the spirit of error. 7Beloved, let us love one another: for love is of GOD; and every one that loveth is born of GOD, and knoweth GOD. 8He that loveth not knoweth not GOD; for GOD is LOVE.

I will not lie to you children, I am GOD. This world will not be a place that you will want to remain behind in to see the outcome of this event. You will not survive what is coming if you want to remain with ME. All those who profess ME after MY bride is removed will die for their faith. It will be a hard time for MY children.

Do not be foolish thinking otherwise.

2 Timothy 3:12. Yea, and all that will live godly in CHRIST JESUS shall suffer persecution.

I will not be mocked. This world cannot continue on in the same vein and believe there are no consequences. I am tired of protecting and caring for a world that hates ME so and mocks ME. This era is about to come to a close. Soon, I will allow the world to have its way, a world without its GOD holding back the evil that will soon come upon it. The world does not value ME as its GOD, so I will let it have its greatest desire, to run itself apart from a HOLY GOD, its DIVINE COMPASS. Then the world will find out the importance of abiding in MY Rules and Laws and following MY Ways Everlasting.

A world without restraint, that is what MY left behind children will witness. It will be a horrible time for mankind. Do not stay behind. Come to ME now. Do not wait.

Clean yourself in MY Blood and MY Word. Dig deep into the Pages of MY Word.

Repent and surrender your life to ME. Let ME save you from what is coming. I am willing. Time is short. Make haste. This is the hour to run into MY Arms. MY Love waits on you.

Let ME save you from the worst. Come under MY Blood Covering to safety. I am anxious to save.

These Words are True and Pure.

This is your LORD, YAHUSHUA MIGHTY TO SAVE.

CHAPTER 35

THERE IS ABSOLUTELY NO BENEFIT IN CHASING AFTER A DYING WORLD

Let US begin again. Children it is your LORD Speaking to you: MY children, I am coming in short order, so do not become discouraged. This world is running out of time to set things right with ME. Soon those who refuse to make things right with ME through repentance and full surrender will suffer the consequences.

MY opponent is blood thirsty and ruthless. The world will know terror like it has never experienced before. This hour approaches swiftly.

I will not withstand much more from this evil, callous world. I have seen and heard enough. It is a world that rejects its GOD and turns its back to MY Ways and MY Truth.

James 4:4. Ye adulterers and adulteresses know ye not that the friendship of the world is enmity with GOD? Whosoever therefore will be a friend of the world is the enemy of GOD.

Children you are being led by the blind if you continue to run aimlessly after the world. There is absolutely no benefit in chasing after a dying world that lacks a moral compass. You must be realizing this by now. Come to grips with the Truth.

There is no hope for this dead, dying world that rejects its MAKER. You must come to attention. Open your eyes. You are being led astray off MY Narrow Path.

Children, few find this path. Sober up! Clean the matter out of your eyes and pull the scales off of them. Come to ME for SPIRITUAL eyes. Let ME open you up to the Truth.

Stop playing with the enemy as if it is all harmless play. He is deadly, ready to strike you when you least suspect it. You are no match for him apart from ME.

You must come close to ME to be protected. It is only by being near ME that you are safe. It is only by staying in MY Book and forging a close relationship with ME that you will survive. Do you understand this? If you go it alone, you will not make it. Don't delude yourself. Don't be foolish. A man's heart is above all else is deceived. MY enemy is too cunning for you. That is why you can only make it by having a close relationship with ME. If you are close to ME, really close, the enemy does not want to come near ME. Darkness can't stand the Light.

So lay down your plans and your life, and render them over to ME. Let ME take them and make your ashes into beauty. Let ME show you MY Perfect Will for your life. I can do it. I am willing. It is MY Desire for you to be in MY Will for your life. This is MY Desire, to clean you up in MY Blood and bring you close to ME, even as a mother loves her child, I long to care for you.

Isaiah 66:13. As one whom his mother comforteth, so will I comfort you; and ye shall be comforted in Jerusalem.

Matthew 23:37. O Jerusalem, Jerusalem, thou that killest the prophets, and stonest them which are sent unto thee, how often would I have gathered thy children together, even as a hen gathereth her chickens under her wings, and ye would not!

Children this hour approaches of MY Soon Return. You are not watching. You will be left. I am only coming for MY children who care to watch, who desire to seek ME in an intimate way. These are the ones who are coming. All others, sadly, will be left. Many among them will even be lost in sudden destruction.

This is a serious hour and these are serious warnings. Read MY Book, open its pages. Pray for MY SPIRIT to lead you to all Truth.

Time is wasting. Don't spend one more minute chasing after a world that hates ME, your GOD. You are moving in a fatal direction. Come to your senses. Seek ME, seek MY SPIRIT, seek MY FATHER, seek US. WE are ONE and WE long to save you.

The hour has come for MY Soon Arrival. Don't miss MY Rescue.

This is your LORD YAHUSHUA, WHO Loves you dearly.

CHAPTER 36

MANY WHO THINK THEMSELVES READY
ARE FOOLING THEMSELVES

Let US begin, MY daughter (March 4, 2012). Listen carefully as I give you new Words. MY child, it is your LORD. Please write these Words down: The hour is approaching for MY Return, so many are still not watching, so many have their blinders on and refuse to listen to reason. The hour of MY Return is coming swiftly. You must be ready children. You must make ready.

Be alert and watching. This is essential to being prepared. Only those watching will be taken. Only those who care to know about MY Return can be made ready.

Those who care not and do not abide in MY SPIRIT will remain to face the worst.

Many will be surprised that they were left. Many will be shocked that they were not taken, so many who think themselves ready are fooling themselves. They are far from being ready. They are tied up in the things of the world. They have their minds on other things. They do not care to watch for MY Coming. They are preoccupied with themselves and the things of the world. They do not spend time with ME. They are not watching for ME.

They mock and persecute those who do, yet they will be dumbfounded when they are left behind, thinking that they know ME. They do not know ME at all.

They only think they know ME. Their hearts are far from ME. They never come to ME in the secret place. They run to the things of the world. Their eyes are not interested in watching for ME. They love to handle and touch the things of the world.

They plan far into the future. They make plans that will never come to pass. They never inquire of ME about these plans, if they did I would tell them to focus on ME, to come near ME, to lay down their plans and surrender them to ME. This is what I want...a full surrender, to lay your plans at MY Feet, to give ME all of you, even your life, and the plans for your future.

Only I know what the future holds. All the plans that anyone makes can crumble in a moment. Why not let ME put MY Plans for your life in place? I know what's best for you, MY children. I know the beginning from the end. I am the ALPHA and OMEGA.

Revelation 22:13. I am the ALPHA and OMEGA, the BEGINNING and the END, the FIRST and the LAST.

I am the CREATOR of the sun, moon, and stars. Do you not think I can care for you and your future plans? I can usher you into MY Kingdom if you would just give ME your life. I can bring you to peace and safety; carry you out with ME to safety. You can live in peace knowing that MY Plans for your life are perfect and I am strong to deliver.

You can have this security if you are in MY Perfect Will for your life. You do not have to worry another day if you are in MY Will. Release the grip you have on your own ways and plans. They will only lead you to destruction.

Surrender your ALL to ME and step into MY Will, MY Perfect Will. Let the ONE WHO knows the beginning from the end to care for you. I am your GOD Everlasting. I will bring you into MY Everlasting Kingdom. It is yours for the asking.

Revelation 21:6. And HE said unto me, It is done. I am the ALPHA and OMEGA, the BEGINNING and the END. I will give unto him that is athirst of the fountain of the water of life freely.

Surrender, repent, and make ME your own. Get to know ME. I will share MY Heart with you. I long to walk with you; you will never be alone. So the time is now to surrender. This is the hour. This is the time. Choose wisely.

There are so many roads. Only one is the right one, only one is the straight path.

Get to know ME and I will lead you on the straight path. This is MY Desire, to guide you and lead you.

Hebrews 12:13. And make straight paths for your feet, lest that which is lame be turned out of the way; but let it rather be healed.

Soon the clock will strike midnight. Run into MY Arms, Safe Arms. Let ME save you. Choose quickly. It makes ME sad to leave anyone, but the choice is theirs.

Don't hesitate to receive MY Love.

YAHUSHUA GOD of Outrageous Love.

1 John 4:16. And we have known and believed the love that GOD hath to us. GOD is LOVE; and he that dwelleth in LOVE dwelleth in GOD, and GOD in him.

CHAPTER 37

YOU HAVE PRECIOUS LITTLE TIME REMAINING

Let US begin. I will give you more Words: Children, it is I, your LORD and I have Words to give you.

The hour grows late. There is little light left in the day. You need to make ready, be ready as MY Coming is close. It is closing in.

Few are ready and watching. Few care to be ready. Many choose to ignore MY Warnings. Most are complacent about what is coming. This hour is closing in.

I want you to be alert and on your toes. If you are not, you will be caught off guard. If you are not watching, you cannot see what is coming. Only those watching will be on the alert. Only those will have then prepared themselves because they are watching. How can you be prepared if you are not watching? Only those prepared and ready will be going. All others will come up short with their oil lamps half full.

Matthew 25:7-10. 7Then all those virgins arose, and trimmed their lamps. 8And the foolish said unto the wise, Give us of your oil; for our lamps are gone out. 9But the wise answered, saying, Not so; lest there be not enough for us and you: but go ye rather to them that sell, and buy for yourselves. 10And while they went to buy, the bridegroom came; and they that were ready went in with him to the marriage: and the door was shut.

This is not the time to be dozing, MY children. This is not the hour to be sleeping.

I am not coming to get those who will not even stay awake long enough to watch for ME. Those who are asleep when I come will awaken to a living nightmare of what is coming to the earth. What a sad time indeed for MY sleeping church.

Hebrews 9:28. So CHRIST was once offered to bear the sins of many; and unto them that look for HIM shall HE appear the second time without sin unto salvation.

MY children are sound asleep and if they don't awaken soon they will find themselves in the hands of MY enemy. He's ruthless and without compassion or concern for anyone. He only has one thing in mind: power and control. He will reign with an iron fist. I cannot impress on you enough the gravity of what's coming. This is a serious hour, and there are serious things coming to the earth.

I do not delight in telling you these things. I only want to warn you of what is coming because I don't want you to suffer through the devastation that is about to befall the earth.

Come to your senses MY children. Awaken from your slumber, remove your blinders. Come to ME quickly. You have precious little time remaining. You must run to ME quickly. I wish to save you from the worst.

Don't get caught in the storm approaching. Very few are coming out with ME when I remove the bride. Very few have chosen to watch for ME and to prepare themselves by the washing of MY Word and the cleansing of MY Blood. There are no other answers. There is no other way.

Ephesians 5:25-27. 25Husbands, love your wives, even as CHRIST also loved the church, and gave HIMSELF for it; 26That HE might sanctify and cleanse it with the washing of water by the Word, 27That HE might present it to HIMSELF a glorious church, not having spot, or wrinkle, or any such thing; but that it should be holy and without blemish.

Surrender this hour. I am ready to receive you. I want you to come to ME and be safe. I will cover you and protect you from the horrors to come. Save yourself and come to ME. I am the only escape—no other exists. Render your heart and your life to ME in a full surrender. You will be made ready, ready by the Work of MY HOLY SPIRIT. Let HIM fill you and you will see the Truth, MY Truth.

I am ready to bring you to MY Kingdom. Are you coming? This is your LORD YAHUSHUA. I Am Patient and Longsuffering Waiting for you to decide. Choose for ME and be saved!

CHAPTER 38

MY TRUE FOLLOWERS ARE WATCHING
- THEY ARE ON GUARD

Daughter Let US begin. MY daughter, I am ready to give you new Words: Children, it is your LORD Speaking. The hour approaches for MY Return and MY children are asleep, they sleep soundly. They are dozing away totally oblivious to what is going on around them. They are not even watching. Clearly they are blind and do not have their eyes on ME.

I will come as a thief in the night. Many will be caught off guard. Doesn't MY Word say it is so? If this is so, why are so many ignoring this warning? Why do they refuse to watch and pay attention? I want their best and they give me their last.

If MY children followed ME closely, they would know to be watching, looking, and waiting for ME. They would be cognizant of the world around them and the way the world is resoundly rejecting ME on all four corners.

MY true followers are watching. They are on guard. They have their ears to the ground and listening for MY Foot Steps. They are watching MY Every Move and they hear MY Voice.

I am coming and this is not a mystery to those who are watching for ME expectantly. These children are patient, yet anxious. This is MY true church, MY bride. She is stunning and her enthusiasm for MY Return is captivating ME. I love her eagerness as she waits for ME. This is who I died for, MY faithful followers who die to themselves for ME.

Luke 12:37. Blessed are those servants, whom the LORD when HE cometh shall find watching: verily I say unto you, that HE shall gird HIMSELF, and make them to sit down to meat, and will come forth and serve them.

They lay down their lives at MY Feet and walk away from the world and the things of the world for their LORD. For this I am most grateful and the rewards will never end for this beautiful church of MINE.

You can be part of this church, MY bride. You can be ready to go, when WE leave together, to the mansions in MY heavenlies I have prepared. There is however precious little time remaining, so be vigilant in your pursuit of ME.

I am looking for a full surrender. I am asking for a full commitment. Lay your life down for ME in all its fullness leaving nothing back. I want your entire life. I will exchange it for a new life in ME. I want to bring you new life. I want to wash you clean in MY Blood; establish you in MY Kingdom; give you a place among MY children who will serve ME for eternity; and rule and reign forever with ME, along aside ME.

This is MY bride. She is beautiful, a prepared people who are ready, waiting, watching for their KING. I am coming to rescue these children, take them out to freedom and safety away from the evils about to overwhelm the earth. They are MY overcomers. You can be among them. I am waiting on you, MY children, to join MY Wedding Party, to be part of MY Kingdom. I am holding a place for you at MY Marriage Supper Table. There is a place setting for you, but you must come and claim it as yours first.

I will not hold the door open forever. Soon, I will bring MY children who are ready through this safe passageway and then it will close leaving those, who refuse MY Invitation to come, behind to face the worst.

What a sad day for those who reject MY Offer of safety and rescue. Their realization on that day of what has happened and what they have missed will be devastating. Then reality will set in as to what they have lost and what they must face. There will be large regrets. There will be much weeping and wailing as MY lukewarm church comes to terms over their sad choices of rejecting and ignoring MY Many Warnings.

Yes, their loss will be enormous and their grief great. Children, this does not have to be you. You do not have to be left to see the darkness enfold around the earth. Come to ME in a full surrender, full repentance, and sincere regret for your sins, and an earnest desire to follow ME with all your heart.

I will change your heart and wash your sin stains white with MY Blood. You will stand before ME prepared and made ready to join MY Great Marriage Supper.

This is the longing of MY Heart for you to come back to ME. I am your FATHER, your CREATOR. I long for you to come to ME, so I can make you MY OWN son and daughter. This is your chance to make things right with ME. Let US live together for eternity. I wait for your decision.

I am your LORD I am your KING I am your GOD JEHOVAH.

CHAPTER 39

MY TESTIMONY:
REGARDING THIS DOCUMENT AND MY FASTING

The LORD called for me to go to a secluded location for prayer and a forty-day water fast. After two weeks, I took communion each day, and a little while later, I took four-four oz. glasses of juice daily. This fast was the most difficult thing I think I have ever done in my life.

The LORD brought me to this fast to die to myself, which I did. HE also gave me many Words which I tried faithfully to record for others to read. The document was dictated to me by the LORD during the days of my fast from January 27, 2012 to March 6, 2012. (Please note that most of the individual Letters dictated to me by the LORD were not individually dated because the fast was so difficult for me, that I did not like to focus on what the dates were or how slow the time of the fast seemed to be going.) During this fast, the LORD told me to ask for "HEAVENLY BREAD" anytime I wanted it to help me with my hunger pains. So I did ask for it whenever I felt hunger pains or any pains associated with fasting. Every time I asked for the "HEAVENLY BREAD" from the LORD, the pains would just simply disappear.

It was amazing and miraculous. The LORD is the "HEAVENLY BREAD" (see the scripture below).

About halfway into the fast, I was reading a book that really made me sit up and take notice. It was about a woman who had been shown heaven and hell. She reported that in hell, those there are eternally hungry and thirsty. This was a defining moment for me during this fast because I was only fasting from food for forty days (and I, of course, was not thirsty because I drank water during this fast) but I could not imagine spending eternity being hungry (when forty-days was an incredible struggle) and thirsty and so I want others to think about this profound truth and to consider seriously about their eternal outcomes.

I am thankful to the LORD for getting me through this forty-day fast.

Regarding these Words given to me, the LORD used many words that I didn't even know the meanings of and I had to look them up and they always were the perfect words. I also am a writer and when I write something as lengthy as this 100-plus page document, then had I written it myself, it would have required me to make many rewrites, edits, deletions, additions and this document was never once altered or changed—I was literally taking down the LORD's Dictation as it was told to me. I wrote the LORD's Words in a journal and retyped it in its entirety without one single rewrite or alteration— perfect English. To GOD be ALL the GLORY! Thank you LORD for your patience with this inferior vessel, Susan Davis.

JESUS IS The HEAVENLY BREAD:

John 6:29-58. 29JESUS answered and said unto them, This is the Work of GOD, that ye believe on HIM whom HE hath sent. 30They said therefore unto HIM, What sign shewest THOU then, that we may see, and believe THEE? What dost THOU Work? 31Our fathers did eat manna in the desert; as it is written, HE gave them bread from Heaven to eat. 32Then JESUS said unto them, Verily, verily, I say unto you, Moses gave you not that bread from Heaven; but MY FATHER giveth you the True BREAD from Heaven. 33For the BREAD of GOD is HE which cometh down from Heaven, and giveth life unto the world. 34Then said they unto HIM, LORD, evermore give us this BREAD.

35And JESUS said unto them, I am the BREAD of LIFE: he that cometh to ME shall never hunger; and he that believeth on ME shall never thirst. 36But 37All I said unto you, That ye also have seen ME, and believe not. That the FATHER giveth ME shall come to ME; and him that cometh to ME I will in no wise cast out. 38For I came down from Heaven, not to do MINE OWN Will, but the Will of HIM that sent ME. 39And this is the FATHER's Will which hath sent ME, that of all which HE hath given ME I should lose nothing, but should raise it up again at the last day. 40And this is the Will of HIM that sent ME, that every one which seeth the SON, and believeth on

HIM, may have everlasting life: and I will raise him up at the last day. 41The Jews then murmured at HIM, because HE said, I am the BREAD which came down from Heaven. 42And they said, Is not this JESUS, the SON of Joseph, whose father and mother we know? How is it then that HE saith, I came down from Heaven? 43JESUS therefore answered and said unto them, Murmur not among yourselves. 44No man can come to ME, except the FATHER which hath sent ME draw him: and I will raise him up at the last day.

45It is written in the prophets, And they shall be all taught of GOD. Every man therefore that hath heard, and hath learned of the FATHER, cometh unto ME. 46Not that any man hath seen the FATHER, save HE which is of GOD, HE hath seen the FATHER. 47Verily, verily, I say unto you, He that believeth on ME hath everlasting life.

48I am that BREAD of LIFE. Your fathers did eat manna in the wilderness, and are dead. 50This is the BREAD which cometh down from Heaven, that a man may eat thereof, and not die. 51I am the LIVING BREAD which came down from Heaven: if any man eat of this BREAD, he shall live for ever: and the BREAD that I will give is MY Flesh, which I will give for the life of the world. 52The Jews therefore strove among themselves, saying, How can this MAN give us HIS Flesh to eat? 53Then JESUS said unto them, Verily, verily, I say unto you, Except ye eat the Flesh of the SON of man, and drink HIS Blood, ye have no life in you. 54Whoso eateth MY Flesh, and drinketh MY Blood, hath eternal life; and I will raise him up at the last day. 55For MY Flesh is meat indeed, and MY Blood is drink indeed. 56He that eateth MY Flesh, and drinketh MY Blood, dwelleth in ME, and I in him. 57As the Living FATHER hath sent ME, and I 49Your live by the FATHER: so he that eateth ME, even he shall live by ME. 58This is that BREAD which came down from Heaven: not as your fathers did eat manna, and are dead: he that eateth of this BREAD shall live for ever.

E-BOOKS FREE !

As well as this book you are now reading, Susan has also co-authored other books about the end-times – also in prophetic form (as received from the Lord) in the "I Am Coming" letters in e-book and printed form. The LORD JESUS' "I Am Coming" letters are available in six volumes:

I AM COMING! Volume 1, Parts 1 to 32, E-book:

http://www.mediafire.com/file/lfyg4uzenfnf6uu/IAmComing1.pdf

I AM COMING! Volume 2, Parts 33 to 52, E-book:

http://www.mediafire.com/file/aywqke1g0cr4rwa/IAmComing2.pdf

I AM COMING! Volume 3, Parts 53 to 73, E-book:

http://www.mediafire.com/file/mdma55jzcwbwpqy/IAmComing3.pdf

I AM COMING! Volume 4, Parts 74 to 96, E-book:

http://www.mediafire.com/file/92y16258w03j0t4/IAmComing4.pdf

I AM COMING! Volume 5, Parts 97 to 122, E-book:

http://www.mediafire.com/file/77n7ynr66o6qlrq/IAmComing5.pdf

I AM COMING! Volume 6, Parts 123 to 139, E-book:

http://www.mediafire.com/file/8vhwt6l4frgh25a/IAmComing6.pdf

Free e-books are also at: http://www.SmashWords.com

Search for: I Am Coming by Susan Davis